Worship Resources for Youth

By
Jerry O. Cook

This book is dedicated to Allison, Elizabeth, and Katharine,
who make my life a joyous celebration.

TABLE OF CONTENTS

FOREWORD

"Why are our youth group's worship services so dull?" "How can I improve our youth worship services?" "What can we do to make worship lively and meaningful for our youth?"

During more than twenty years of working with church youth groups and leading seminars for adult workers with youth, I have heard these questions again and again. For many—perhaps most—church youth groups, worship is the weakest part of the youth program. Even those groups that have scintillating discussions of the faith, exciting service projects, and fun-filled recreation periods are often at a loss when it comes to planning and experiencing meaningful worship services.

The problem is many-faceted. In many cases, young people and their adult leaders do not have sufficient knowledge of either the theology of worship or the components of a good worship service. Moreover, they are hampered by their lack of knowledge of good worship resources. And, to compound matters even further, there simply are not that many good worship resources available. Is it any wonder, then, that youth worship services tend to be a mish-mash of poorly correlated prayers, songs, and homilies gleaned from devotional books and other resources?

This book is an attempt to fill that double void caused by lack of knowledge and lack of resources. **Part One** deals with the overall picture by providing suggestions regarding planning and leading youth worship services, some basic information on worship theology and the components of worship services, and some hints on using this book. **Part Two** contains forty-five "model services" and suggestions for ways in which you may alter or adapt most of these services. **Part Three** includes some original folk hymns and service music, a guide to ordering movies, and an annotated listing of additional resources.

I have written this book in response to an urgent need that I have heard expressed by youth workers all over the country. I have also written it *for myself*! In working with youth in local churches, I have been frustrated by the lack of a comprehensive one-volume resource for youth worship. This book is an attempt to alleviate that frustration for all of us. I hope that it will be an invaluable aid for you as you try to help young people discover the joy and the strength that may be found in meaningful worship of Almighty God!

Grace and peace,

Jerry O. Cook
Brewster, Massachusetts
Summer 1983

For information write:
   Rev. Steven E. Clapp
   C-4 RESOURCES
   P.O. Box 1408
   Champaign, IL 61820

Printing and Assembly by Crouse Printing of Champaign, Illinois.
Special thanks to: David and Shirley Crouse, Steve Askins, Sonnie Schrock, Beth Sholar, Ralph Crabtree, Ed Anderson and Nan Craig.

ISBN 0-914527-01-0

PART ONE: INTRODUCTION

THE TEAM APPROACH TO WORSHIP

This book is designed to be used by teams of youth *and* adults. Its approach is based on the assumption that worship, like other aspects of youth ministry, is most effective when it is a *joint endeavor* of the young people and their adult leaders. The reason for this assumption? Youth need the guidance and maturity that adult leaders can provide; and adults need the special perspectives and insights that can be provided by young people.

How much guidance and direction should adults provide? The answer to this question depends to a great extent on the level of maturity and the amount of knowledge evidenced by the youth with which the adults are working. Some young people need a lot of supervision; others are quite able to take initiative and carry out tasks almost entirely on their own. Thus, a good adult leader will get to know the young people's abilities, so that he or she can avoid either stifling creativity and effort through too much guidance or allowing chaos and ineffectiveness by not providing enough guidance.

As a general rule, older teenagers require less direction and guidance than do younger teenagers. With a group of young junior highs, for example, the adult leader would probably take much of the initiative and provide quite a bit of supervision. With older senior highs, on the other hand, the adult leader would probably want to give the young people a great deal of responsibility for planning, leading, and evaluating the worship experiences. Nevertheless, this general rule is only a guiding principle. The primary criterion should always be the question of the individual group's level of maturity and ability.

It is recommended that worship teams be involved in a time-tested procedure known as "the P-I-E process." This process has three parts: (1) Planning; (2) Implementation; and (3) Evaluation. All three of these elements are essential if a group is to have meaningful and interesting worship experiences.

Here are some things to consider in each step of this process:

Planning. With few exceptions, worship services should be carefully planned well in advance. Although some extemporaneous worship services may be exciting and effective, this is not generally the case. There is usually a direct ratio between the amount of planning and the effectiveness of the service.

Good planning involves two phases. **First,** there should be a long-range planning session in which the team makes plans for an extended period of time, usually a month or a quarter. During this session, the team should decide on the theme or basic approach for a group of services. Once the overall emphasis is determined, the team should then decide on sub-topics that will be dealt with in the individual services for this extended period of time. Then the team should begin to do some basic brainstorming about Scripture, music, prayers, and so forth for the services. At this point, plans should also be made for ordering films, securing guest speakers, and taking care of other advance-planning matters.

The **second** phase of worship planning involves a detailed consideration of the components of the individual services. Usually, this planning takes place on a weekly basis.

Among the questions to be considered in these sessions are the following:

- What is the primary theme of the service?
- What do we want people to do as a result of their participation in the service?
- What Scriptures, songs, prayers, creeds, and so forth, will be used in the service?
- Does the team want to amplify the service by adding additional components (like those suggested in the section "Additional Ideas for This Service" in most of the services in this book)? If so, who will take responsibility for these special additions? What guidance will these persons need?
- Who will lead the various parts of the service? What guidance will these persons need? Is it necessary to rehearse the service? If so, how will this rehearsal be carried out?
- Who will provide musical accompaniment? Who will lead the singing? What guidance will these persons need?
- Will audio-visual equipment, films, recordings, and so forth, be used? Have films and other materials been secured in advance? Who will be responsible for checking the condition of machines and operating machines? What guidance is needed for these persons?

Implementation. The leading of the service is a simple matter if proper preparation has been made ahead of time. Nevertheless, there are some important logistical matters to consider. Here are some hints that will help worship leaders be effective:

- Speak in a loud, clear voice. Talk at a moderate pace—not too slowly and not too fast.
- Use simple, "non-flowery" rubrics (directions for the worshipers). As a rule, these should be expressed in proper style (for example, "Let us pray" rather than "May we pray?" and "Let us worship with our offerings" rather than a wordy statement like "It's now time for us to show our appreciation for our many God-given blessings by sharing a portion of our bounty here at the divine altar").

- Sing hymns and songs at the proper tempo. Avoid rushing or dragging the music.
- Move from one part of the service to another with as little disruption as possible. Try to have audio-visual selections ready to go without unnecessary moving of equipment.
- Be reverent, but avoid being stiff and overly formal.
- Keep the worshipers' attention directed toward the worship of God. Avoid "hamming it up" and spotlighting the worship leaders.

Evaluation. No youth ministry experience is complete without an evaluation. Take a few minutes after the service to meet as a team and evaluate the worship experience. Then consider ways in which your evaluation may be helpful to you as you plan the next service.

Here are some questions to consider in your evaluation:

- Were worship leaders effective in leading the service? Why or why not?
- Did all the worshipers participate fully in the service? Why or why not?
- Which parts of the service were most effective? Why? Which parts were least effective? Why?
- If you could do this service over, what would you change? Why?
- What did you learn from this service that could help you in planning and leading future services? How will you implement these learnings?

A BASIC THEOLOGY OF WORSHIP

The Meaning and Purpose of Worship. People have many and varying ideas about what worship is all about. Some people feel that the purpose of worship is to give the worshiper a good feeling, a feeling of comfort and reassurance about life. Others feel that a worship service should inspire the worshiper; they believe that one should come away from worship with a "high," an exalted feeling resulting from a "mountaintop experience." Still others feel that the purpose of worship is to help people become more conscious of their responsibility to live Christ-like lives of service to other people.

While all these ideas are certainly commendable, they do not focus on the central purpose and meaning of worship. *In fact, they misplace the emphasis of worship by focusing on the worshiper rather than on God.* Whatever happens to the worshiper in a worship service is a by-product. The main purpose of worship is not to produce a particular feeling or experience for the worshiper, regardless of how important such a result may be for the worshiper's own personal life. **The main purpose of worship is to praise and glorify God!** And true worship occurs when our attention and our efforts are focused on this goal. Ironically, all the good things that happen to *us* in worship occur most dramatically and most forcibly when we participate in a service that is directed toward proclaiming God's glory and greatness!

Worship is itself an interesting word. Its history tells us a lot about the meaning and purpose of worship. According to the dictionary, the word "worship" comes from the Old English word *weorthscipe*, which we may translate into modern English as "worth-ship." In a properly-focused worship service, what we do is to affirm God's "worth-ship" for our lives. We declare the value and meaning that God has for us.

In any worship service, there is, of course, a time for examining our own lives, for discovering how our lives could be changed and improved. But this worshiper-oriented aspect is secondary. And in order for it to occur in ways that are deep and lasting, it must happen in the context of an experience that focuses on the centrality of God in our lives.

The Components of a Worship Service. Let's look at what happens in a typical worship service. Although most worship services may have a dozen or so parts, there are five basic categories for describing the actions that occur in a typical service. Fortunately, these five categories form an acronym—A-C-T-E-D—which makes it easy for us to remember the basic components of worship!

A—Worship is first, and primarily, **Adoration and Praise of God!** Regardless of whatever personal agendas *we* may bring to worship, the main purpose of worship is to praise God. For this reason, we should always open a worship service by focusing on God. Usually, we begin with the minister or some other person calling the people to direct their attention to the value of God for their lives. Strictly speaking, this "call to worship" is not a part of the worship service itself, but rather a prologue to worship. In some churches, the musical prelude and the call to worship are listed separately at the beginning under a heading such as "The Service of Gathering."

The actual worship service itself really begins with the first statement of praise, usually a hymn, which is sometimes designated as "The Hymn of Praise." In many hymnals, these hymns of praise are printed at the beginning of the hymnal to emphasize their place at the beginning of worship.

The opening of the service often includes other elements that enable us to praise God. Typical of these are affirmations of faith, praise-oriented Psalms, and canticles of praise such as theDoxology or the Gloria Patri.

C—Once we have declared our praise of God, we are ready for step two—**Confession.** As we affirm God's value for our lives, we become conscious of our failure to keep our part of the covenantal relationship that God has established with us. We realize that in many ways we have failed to do God's will and that we have done things that are contrary to God's will. So we make a confession of our failures, and we ask for God's forgiveness.

Confessional prayers are of two basic types: (1) the prayer of reflection, in which the worshipers meditate on the spiritual state of their lives; and (2) the prayer of confession of sins, in which the worshipers confess sins and ask for forgiveness. The first type of prayer may be used alone, with no follow-up statement. In the case of the second type, however, the prayer should *always* be followed with words of hope and assurance, so that worshipers may be assured that they are freed from guilt and enabled to lead new lives in Christ!

T—Having examined our spiritual state and having realized that God forgives and accepts us, we come naturally to the third part of the drama of worship—**Thanksgiving.** In the main act of thanksgiving, we bring our offering of money to the altar of God and thank God for loving and caring for us.

In many of the services in this book, the offering of gifts is an optional part of the services, since many youth groups do not give offerings on a regular basis. Nevertheless, the act of thanksgiving is an important component of worship; and, even when no offering of money is made, it is always appropriate to have a period when prayers of thanksgiving may be offered.

E—A fourth category of worship actions includes our discussion of the ways in which the word of God relates to our lives. This category is sometimes designated by the term **Education**, but it may also be designated by other "E words": Enlightenment; Edification; Elucidation. This category is often called "The Service of the Word," since it includes worship actions that help us relate the Bible to our lives.

In most churches, the main actions under this category are the Scripture readings, a hymn of preparation, and the sermon. For many congregations, another important element in this category is the stating of concerns and celebrations—those aspects of peoples' lives that need to be looked at by the worshiping community.

In the regular weekly services provided in this book, a central part of the education component is what we have designated as the "Probe of the Word"—an activity that helps worshipers relate the Scriptural message to their lives.

D—The final category of worship actions is **Dedication.** No worship service is complete without a response by the people. This response may take many forms. In some churches, it centers on an "altar call," by which the people are invited to come to the altar and renew their lives. In other traditions, it may simply consist of a hymn of dedication. In some congregations, there is also a responsive "act of dedication," by which the worship leader and the people affirm their renewed dedication to God's will for their lives. Also included in this category is the benediction or blessing, a prayer in which the worship leader and/or the people ask for God's blessing as they go forth to live their lives in the light of their renewed dedication to God.

Most services contain all five of the A-C-T-E-D element. Often, but not always, these elements occur in the order in which they appear in the acronym. In some cases, certain elements are deliberately omitted, as in the Easter and Christmas services, for example, in which some traditions omit the act of confession in order to focus the whole service on God's action in Christ. In some instances, churches that ordinarily employ these five elements in their traditional order may vary the order for very good reasons, as in a Good Friday service, for example, when the service begins with confession in order to emphasize the penitential nature of the worship experience.

Most of the services in this book utilize these five elements in their traditional order, although we have not made it a hard-and-fast rule to do so. In some cases, when it is appropriate to make changes from traditional practice, we have not hesitated to vary the order and/or delete one or more of the basic five elements.

The above discussion on worship theology is adapted from the chapter entitled "Worship" in the book **Youth Workers' Handbook** *by Steve Clapp and Jerry O. Cook (C-4 Resources, 1983). For a more detailed discussion on worship theology and additional ideas on helping young people to learn about worship, you may wish to read this chapter (pages 227-237) in its entirety.*

THE WORSHIP SERVICES IN THIS BOOK

The central part of this book contains materials for forty-five worship services. The first forty services are designed to be used by a youth group during its regular weekly meetings. These services are arranged so that they roughly parallel the September-June portion of the standard church year—with seasonal and other special services marked with sub-titles. With very little rearranging of the order in which these services appear, you could use the first service on the Sunday after Labor Day and continue right through the series—with the last service being used sometime mid-June. This arrangement was chosen only as a matter of convenience, however. You should feel free to pick and choose among these forty services at any time in order to find one that is appropriate for any particular meeting. You should also feel free to create new services by combining individual parts from various services.

Each service in this section consists of two parts. **First,** there is an introductory section which itself contains two parts: "Guidelines for the Basic Service" and "Additional Ideas for This Service." **Second,** there is a basic model service which can be used just as it is given.

"Guidelines for the Basic Service." This section contains suggestions for using the model service. Included in these guidelines are the following sub-sections:

Purpose. A statement of the purpose of the model service.

Resources and Materials Needed. A listing of resources and materials that will be needed for the model service. These items should be secured prior to the service.

Hymns. A statement about the hymns suggested for the model service. Since most standard hymns were written years before the present-day discussions about sexist language, many of these hymns contain references to "man" and "mankind" and other words that do not reflect the modern concern for "inclusive" language. Wherever it is possible to make alterations without destroying the metrical patterns of hymn verses, we suggest changes in wording in order to make hymns more inclusive.

One exception to our general procedure should be noted. We have refrained from indiscriminately changing such traditional terms as "Lord" and "Father." Contemporary concern about sexist language has made us aware that the feminine aspects of God also deserve emphasis. And it is certainly true that persons who have had bad experiences with their fathers may have trouble identifying with God as "Father." Nevertheless, it is impossible to talk about God without using symbols. The use of "Father" for God and "Lord" for God or Christ is a tradition that runs through the Scriptures. For the most part, we have chosen not to change those hymns which contain such Biblical titles.

Offering and Doxology. With few exceptions, the statements about these worship components point out that they are optional and refer you to ideas on Doxologies in Part Three of this book.

Scripture. This section gives a brief explanatory statement about the scriptural selection(s) used in the model service. Use the ideas in this statement in preparing persons for the Probe of the Word. Also included in this section is a statement about preferred translations. As a general rule, it is suggested that you use *Today's English Version (TEV)*, which is a clear, understandable translation. In some instances, the service recommends reading from the *Revised Standard Version (RSV)*.

The *Today's English Version* is less sexist than most. In certain instances, we would suggest for making the language less sexist and more inclusive. Although some persons may be bothered by such changes in Scripture, it should be pointed out that the Bible is a book for and about *all* people and that the practice of making such alterations as changing "he" to "he or she" and "man" to "person" does not represent disrespect for the Scripture but rather an attempt to make the Bible more relevant to all persons—male and female. This practice is now standard procedure for many pastors when they read Scripture aloud in worship, and it is quite probable that future translations of the Bible will reflect this type of sensitivity to the need for inclusive language.

Probe of the Word. This section describes a unique feature of these model services. Rather than include a sermon or homily, we have chosen to suggest some interesting and creative methods for delving into the ways in which the Scripture affects our lives. These probes of the word take many forms: activities, questionnaires, skits, and so forth. They are designed to draw students into interesting encounters with the Scripture. You may choose to use these probes as they are, to alter or adapt them, or to substitute entirely different methods for making God's Word come alive. If you decide to substitute a sermon or a meditation, that's fine, too! There's nothing wrong with a verbal interpretation of the Bible's message for us. But, for those who want a *different* way of exploring the Scripture in a worship service, we think that the probe approach will be exciting and rewarding!

"Additional Ideas for This Service." This section contains suggestions for altering and/or amplifying the model service. It is designed to give you some creative ideas and also to help spark your own creativity.

The additional ideas suggested in these sections are numerous, varied, and far-ranging. Although it is difficult to summarize the contents of these sections within the confines of this introduction, the following information will give you some indication of the types of ideas that these sections contain:

Hymns. This section suggests standard hymns and folk hymns (our term for folk-type hymns and "religious" popular songs) that may be used in addition to and/or instead of the hymns in the model services. The suggested standard hymns may be found in denominational and ecumenical hymnals. The folk-type hymns may be found in the various songbooks cited as sources—with bibliographical information on these sognbooks given in Part Three of this book. Whenever popular songs are suggested, publishers and dates of publication are given immediately following the titles of the songs.

Movies. This section contains basic information on movies that may be used in the services. Information on ordering these movies is given in the "Movies" section in Part Three of this book.

Recorded Music. This section contains information on recorded music that may be used as preludes, offertories, postludes, calls to worship, benedictions, and so forth. In some cases, suggestions are also given for ways in which these musical selections may be used in slide-and-tape presentations.

Miscellaneous Additional Ideas. Many miscellaneous suggestions for enhancing worship are included in the additional-idea sections. These suggestions are numerous and varied. Examples are: ideas on using a shofar (Jewish ram's horn) in worship; suggestions on how to "pass the peace" in worship; ideas on the usage of Advent wreaths; and ideas on the use of dramatic selections.

The Model Service. This section consists of an order of worship for a basic service. The service is designed so that it can be utilized with only a minimum of preparation.

Each of these services is organized around a central theme (as indicated in the service title). Hymns, Scriptures, prayers, word-probes, and other service elements are arranged in such a way as to provide a logical "flow" in the services—with each part of the service emphasizing and developing the service's main idea.

Obviously, the model services can be "lifesavers" for those meetings when you do not have much time for preparation. They should not be seen only as a course of last resort, however! Careful thought and preparation have gone into the designing of these services, and—although worship is generally enriched by additional creative ideas—the model services can be quite effective if used just as they are!

Special Services for Camps and Retreats. These two services are designed to be used in special settings; they are particularly appropriate for outdoor worship services. Since these services are for special-event occasions rather than for regular weekly meetings, the services include components necessitating the use of special resources and materials. You should feel free, of course, to make deletions, additions, or other alterations in order to adapt these services for your own situation.

Youth-Led Services for Congregational Worship. These three services are designed to be used on those occasions when your youth group has the opportunity to lead worship for the entire congregation. Included in this section are two seasonal services and a standard congregational worship service. Here again, as in the services for camps and retreats, you should feel free to delete, add, or alter in other ways in order to adapt these services for your own situation.

Permission to Photocopy the Material in This Book

Our intention in this book is to provide you with youth worship resources at minimal cost! Therefore, you have permission—*carte blanche*, unqualified, and absolute—to copy anything in this book for use in your youth group. Once you purchase one copy of the book, you have permission to copy anything in the book (including the copyrighted music) by Xeroxing, mimeographing, or any other method! If you want to purchase more than one copy, that's fine, too; but you don't *have* to buy multiple copies. Be our guest! The book is yours to copy to your heart's content; and it's all legal and ethical—as long as you buy at least one copy of the book for your group!

PART TWO: WORSHIP SERVICES

WORSHIP SERVICES FOR WEEKLY YOUTH GROUP MEETINGS

WORSHIP SERVICE NO. 1: "BECOMING A GROUP"

Guidelines for the Basic Service

Purpose: To enable persons to experience group-building in a worship service.

Resources and Materials Needed: Bibles; hymnals; a pencil and a piece of paper for each participant.

Hymns. The two suggested hymns are found in many hymnals. Alternative ideas are given in "Additional Ideas for This Service."

Offering and Doxology. This section is optional. For ideas on Doxologies, see "Additional Hymns and Service Music" in Part Three of this book.

Scripture. Matthew 18:19-20 gives us Jesus' promise to be in our midst when we gather in His name. This passage also promises that God will hear our prayers when *we* agree on what we are praying for. Romans 12:4-5 points out that Christians of differing backgrounds and abilities can be "members one of another" when they share together as a Christian group. Second Corinthians 5:16-20 provides words of hope and reconciliation. Numbers 6:24-26 is a benediction that is used by many youth groups. The RSV translation is recommended for the first three Scriptures and the TEV for the fourth.

Probe of the Word. This part of the service is designed to help members of the group become better acquainted with one another. Some persons may be reluctant to talk about their own talents and abilities, so you will need to assure them in advance that there is nothing wrong with affirming the gifts that God has given them. Let them know that this activity is not a means of "tooting their own horns," but rather a means of expressing their appreciation for the uniqueness that God has given them. Be sure to emphasize the young persons' special talents and abilities in the group sharing-time.

Additional Ideas for This Service

If you have additional time and/or resources, you may wish to consider some of the following suggestions for alteration of the basic service:

Hymns. Substitute standard hymns or folk hymns for those suggested in the basic service. Alternatives for the *first* hymn: (1) *Standard Hymns:* "All Praise to Our Redeeming Lord"; (2) *Folk Hymns:* "They'll Know We Are Christians by Our Love" (*Songbook for Saints and Sinners, The Genesis Songbook,* and other collections); "Psalm of Thanksgiving" (*Exodus Songbook*).

Alternatives for the *second* hymn: (1) *Standard Hymns:* "O Shepherd of the Nameless Fold"; "Jesus, Lord, We Look to Thee"; "Jesus, With They Church Abide"; (2) *Folk Hymns:* "I Believe in Your" (*Close Your Eyes; I Got a Surprise*); "I'd Like to Teach the World to Sing" (*The Genesis Songbook*).

Movies. You may wish to use a movie on the theme of unity. Suggestions are: (1) *Baptism: Sacrament of Belonging* (16mm, color. 8 minutes, produced by Franciscan Communications Center). The story of how a community of Christian children accepts Alfredo, a homeless boy with a fire-scarred face. (2) *Nail* (16mm, color, 20 minutes, produced by Family Films). A modern parable that shows how a nail in a pot of soup water helps alienated apartment dwellers find fellowship and community.

For information on film rentals, see "Movies" in Part Three of this book.

ORDER OF WORSHIP

Call to Worship *(responsively)*
Welcome to this group!
Thanks! We are happy to be here!
Why *are* you here?
We are here to worship God and to seek the unity that God can give to us.
Then let us praise God and ask God to be in our midst so that we may become a caring Christian community.

Hymn: "From All That Dwell Below The Skies"

Prayer of Confession *(unison)*
O God, we know that you want us to be friends with one another. We are aware that you would like for all people to live in peace and harmony.
Forgive us for the hard feelings that ruin friendships,
   for the failure to listen to and understand one another,
   for the pride that widens the gaps among us.
Help us to overcome our differences rather than emphasizing them.
Help us truly to understand one another, so that we may love one another and become a real Christian group—through Christ our true friend. Amen.

Words of Hope and Forgiveness: 2 Corinthians 5:16-20
(to be said by the worship leader)

Offering and Doxology

Scripture: Matthew 18:19-20; Romans 12:4-5

Probe of the Word: Getting to Know One Another
Hand out pencils and pieces of paper. Have each person take a few minutes to answer the following questions:

1. What is your name?
2. In what way(s) are you a special and unique person?
3. What experience that you have had during the past few months would you like to share with the group?
4. Why are you attending today's meeting of this group?
5. What significant contributions do you feel that you can make to this group during the next few months?

Afterward, have persons share their responses in teams of two or three. Then have persons use the information that they received in the teams to introduce their team partners to the group as a whole. Close by having a prayer in which you ask God to mold you into a group that cares for and affirms its individual members.

Hymn: "Blest Be the Tie That Binds"

Benediction: Numbers 6:24-26 *(to be prayed by the worship leader)*

WORSHIP SERVICE NO. 2: "CELEBRATING OURSELVES"

Guidelines for the Basic Service

Purpose: To enable persons to celebrate themselves in a worship service.

Resources and Materials Needed: Bibles; hymnals; a pencil and a piece of paper for each participant.

Hymns. The first hymn is found in many hymnals. The folk hymn "A Song to Celebrate Myself" is in "Additional Hymns and Service Music" in Part Three of this book. Alternative ideas are given in "Additional Ideas for This Service."

Offering and Doxology. This section is optional. For ideas on Doxologies, see "Additional Hymns and Service Music" in Part Three of this book.

Scripture. Genesis 1:26-31 states that God created human beings in the image of God. Psalms 8 affirms that human beings are created just a little below God; this psalm thus strongly re-affirms the Genesis passage. It is suggested that you substitute "humanity" or "human beings" for "man" in Psalms 8.

Philippians 3:12-14 affirms a positive view of humanity: Though we are not perfect, we don't dwell on our imperfections but rather press forward to our full potential as found in Jesus Christ.

Probe of the Word. This part of the service is designed to help participants discover their own value and thus learn how to affirm themselves andothers.

Additional Ideas for This Service

If you have additional time and/or resources, you may wish to consider some of the following suggestions for alteration of the basic service:

Movies. You may wish to use one of these movies on the theme of celebration: (1) *How Good Life Can Be* (16mm, color, 30 minutes, produced by Lutheran Brotherhood). (2) *Celebrate Yourself* (16mm, color, 30 minutes, produced by WTVD-TV of Durham, NC). A documentary showing how some handicapped people celebrate life and themselves in worship. Use the song "A Song to Celebrate Myself."

For information on film rentals, see "Movies" in Part Three of this book.

Hymns. Substitute any hymn of praise (usually hymns in first part of church hymnals) for the *first* hymn. Substitute one of these alternatives for the *second* hymn: "I'm OK, You're OK"; "Everything is Beautiful"; "You Are the Salt of the Earth" (all in *Exodus Songbook*); "Thank You, Lord"; "Every Morning Is Easter Morning" (both in *Avery and Marsh Songbook*); "Happiness"; "Anything Happens"; (both in *Wherever You Go*).

Recorded Music. Play "What a Piece of Work Is Man" (from the RCA album *Hair*) immediately after the Probe of the Word. Point out that "man" in the lyrics (by Shakespeare) should be understood as "humanity." Coordinate slides of shots of various people with the song to make an audio-visual presentation. For ideas on making home-made slides and producing slide-and-music presentations, see pages 116-126 of *Youth Workers' Handbook* (C-4 Resources, 1983) or refer to some of the books on audio-visual techniques listed in Part Three of this book.

ORDER OF WORSHIP

Call to Worship *(responsively)*
Who are you?
We are human beings created in the image of God. We are people whom God has made to be just below God in the scale of creation. But sometimes we fail to recognize the potential within us.
Then use your eyes to see and use your ears to hear! Look within yourselves and see the goodness that God has created! Listen to God's voice affirming your worth!
We will try to recognize our value and celebrate our lives.
In that spirit, then, let us worship God our Creator!

Hymn: "Praise to the Living God"

Prayer of Reflection *(unison)*
O God, you see clearly what is within our hearts. You know and accept us as we are. Help us to learn how to deal with our uncertainties about ourselves. Make us aware of the beauty of our God-given souls. Show us the joy, the love, and the sensitivity that are within us. Help us to love and celebrate ourselves—so that we may love and celebrate you, the one who created us. Amen.

Offering and Doxology

Scripture: Genesis 1:26-31; Psalms 8

Probe of the Word: Celebrating Ourselves
Hand out pencils and pieces of paper. Have each person take a few minutes to respond to the following statements:

1. My name is _____

2. My best quality is _____

3. My greatest achievement during the past year was _____

4. I help other people by _____

5. During my lifetime, I will improve the world by _____

Afterward, have each person share what he or she has written. As each person finishes, have the members of the group say aloud in unison: *We celebrate* _____ *who is a good person created in the image of God!*

Scripture: Philippians 3:12-14

Hymn: "A Song to Celebrate Myself"

Benediction *(to be said by the worship leader)*
Go forth as good persons—persons created in God's image. May each of you celebrate yourself as one of God's good gifts to the world. Amen.

WORSHIP SERVICE NO. 3: "AFFIRMING ONE ANOTHER"

Guidelines for the Basic Service

Purpose: To help persons discover in worship how to affirm one another.

Resources and Materials Needed: Bibles; hymnals; "warm fuzzies" (see below)

Hymns. The two suggested hymns are found in many hymnals. Alternative ideas are given in "Additional Ideas for This Service."

Offering and Doxology. This section is optional. For ideas on Doxologies, see "Additional Hymns and Service Music" in Part Three of this book.

Scripture. In John 13:34-35, Jesus gives his "new commandment": Love one another so that people will know that you are Christians. Ephesians 4:29-32 urges Christians to affirm other people and avoid hurtful, harmful words and actions. The TEV is recommended for both readings.

Probe of the Word. Participants (including the worship leader) should be seated in a circle. To make "warm fuzzies," you will need: "fake fur" (or pieces of cloth), small beads, glue, and masking tape. Assemble the "fuzzies" according to this diagram:

WARM FUZZIES

BEADS-APPLY WITH GLUE

TOP VIEW

2"

1"

FAKE FUR

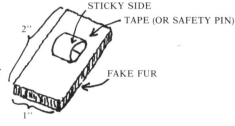

STICKY SIDE

TAPE (OR SAFETY PIN)

2"

BOTTOM VIEW

FAKE FUR

1"

Additional Ideas for This Service

If you have additional time and/or resources, you may wish to consider some of the following suggestions for alteration of the basic service:

Hymns. Substitute standard hymns or folk hymns for those suggested in the basic service. *Standard Hymns:* Any hymns on the theme of Christian love. *Folk Hymns:* "They'll Know We Are Christians by Our Love" (*Songbook for Saints and Sinners, Genersis Songbook*, and other collections); "Sing Love Songs" (*Avery and Marsh Songbook*); "Magic Penny"; "Love One Another"; "I'm OK, You're OK"; "You've Got a Friend"; "What the World Needs Now Is Love" (all in *Exodus Songbook*); "Moments to Live By"; "All I ask of You" (both in *Listen*); "I Believe you You" (*Close Your Eyes, I've Got a Surprise*); "Pass It On" (in the musical *Tell It Like It Is*—Lexicon Music, 1960; also in many song collections); "New Circles" (in "Additional Hymns and Services Music" in Part Three of this book).

Recorded Music. Use one of these recordings as a prelude and the other as a postlude: "Bridge Over Troubled Waters" (from Simon and Garfunkel's album of that name or their *Greatest Hits* album—both by Columbia Records); James Taylor's "Shower the People You Love With Love" (from his Warner album *Greatest Hits*).

Movies. After the Probe of the Word, show one of these movies dealing with the way in which we can affirm and build up other people: (1) *A Fuzzy Tale* (16mm, color, 12 minutes, produced by United Methodist Communications). An animated version of the Claude Steiner story celebrating giving and loving without fear of rejection. (2) *Parable* (16mm, color, 22 minutes, produced by Rolf Forsburg). The classic film about a clown, a Christ-figure who affirms other people and gives meaning to their lives.

For information on film rentals, see "Movies" in Part Three of this book.

ORDER OF WORSHIP

Call to Worship (*responsively*)
The voice of God is calling to us. Will we listen?
We will try to hear God's voice.
The love of God challenges us. Will we accept the challenge?
We will try to be channels of God's love.
God's spirit is seeking us. Will it find us?
We will try to be open to this spirit as it enters our lives.
Let us hear the call. Let us accept the challenge. Let us be open to the spirit—as we worship God together.

Hymn: "Love Divine, All Loves Excelling"

Prayer of Reflection (*unison*)
O God, we are surrounded by people who need us. Some need a comforting word. Some need a tender touch. Some need encouragement and approval. At times we withhold ourselves from those who need us, and we pretend that they are not there. At times we are too busy to notice. Help us to be more sensitive, more caring. Fill us with the loving concern that Jesus showed toward other people. Guide our words and our actions so that we might heal and help, so that we might produce happiness rather than hurt and harm. We pray this prayer in the name of our Lord Jesus Christ, the one affirms us all. Amen.

Scripture: John 13:34-35; Ephesians 4:29-32

Offering and Doxology

Probe of the Word: "Warm Fuzzies"*
Hold up one of the "warm fuzzies." Then say: *All of us like to receive compliments. None of us likes to be insulted or "put down." Every day of our lives we send out positive or negative messages to one another. We do it with words, with gestures, with the expressions on our faces. Some psychologists call these messages "strokes." A man named Carl Steiner created the term "warm fuzzies" to describe positive strokes and the term "cold pricklies" to describe negative strokes. I am going to give each of you a symbolic "warm fuzzy." . . . Take a few minutes to think about the person on your right. Then we will go around the circle, and each of you is to hand the symbolic "warm fuzzy" to the person on your right and then give that person a real "warm fuzzy" in the form of a compliment. Afterward, we will wear our "fuzzies" as symbols to remind us of the obligation that a Christian has to affirm and help others.*
Proceed with the activity as described in your instructions.

Hymn: "Jesus, United by Thy Grace"

Benediction (*to be said by the worship leader*)
Go forth into a world that needs help and healing. Offer to all the comforting word, the approving look, the caring touch—just as Jesus would do. Amen.

---

*You may wish to use in your preparation and/or presentation Claude Steiner's book *A Warm Fuzzy Tale* (Jalmar Press, 1977).

WORSHIP SERVICE NO. 4: "THE BREAD OF THE WORLD"
(World Communion Sunday)

Guidelines for the Basic Service

Purpose: To enable persons to celebrate Communion in worship.

Resources and Materials Needed: Bibles; hymnals; an altar or table (optional); pastries, cakes, or bread (one serving per person); beverage and glasses (one glass per person); food for a snack meal.

Hymns. The two suggested hymns are found in many hymnals. The first hymn is also in many folk hymn collections. Alternative ideas are given in "Additional Ideas for This Service."

Offering and Doxology. This section is optional—but it is preferable that it be included, since an offering and a hymn of praise such as the Doxology should ordinarily be a part of any Communion service. For ideas on Doxologies, see "Additional Hymns and Service Music" in Part Three of this book.

Scripture. The selection from 1 John is one of the classic Biblical statements of assurance of forgiveness. Paul's description of the Lord's Supper in 1 Corinthians 11 is the oldest Communion narrative in the New Testament. The TEV is preferred for both selections.

Probe of the Word. Decide in advance whether you will serve Communion or have participants serve one another. Be sure to check with your minister or priest to see whether your denomination requires that an ordained clergyperson be in charge of all Communion services.

Plan your preliminary meal well in advance. Make sure that you have enough food and drink to serve everyone—*and enough Communion elements!*

Additional Ideas for This Service

If you have additional time and/or resources, you may wish to consider some of the following suggestions for alteration of the basic service:

Hymns. Substitute standard hymns or folk hymns for those suggested in the basic service. *Standard Hymns:* Any Communion hymns. Some possibilities: "Be Known to Us in Breaking Bread"; "Author of Life Divine"; "Hear, O My Lord, I See." *Folk Hymns:* "Welcome" (*Avery and Marsh Songbook*); "We All Stand at Your Table"; "Take and Eat (Re-Member Me)" (both in *A New Commandment*); "Happy Are They"; "In Him We Live" (both in *Abba, Father*); "Take Our Bread"; "Shared Bread"; "Yes to You, My Lord"—change second "brothers" to "sisters"; "Thanks Be to God"—may be sung also to the tune of the old song "Windy" by the group The Association (all in *Songbook for Saints and Sinners*).

An Alternative Musical Service. Use selections from the folk-Communion service *A Celebration of Life* in "Additional Hymns and Service Music" in Part Three of this book.

Passing of the Peace. If you have a particularly open group, you may find shaking hands somewhat stilted and formal. Persons in such groups should feel free to hug one another or even to give one another "the kiss of peace" on the cheek.

Movies. Show one of these movies about Communion just before the Probe of the Word: (1) *Eucharist* (16mm, color, 10 minutes, produced by Franciscan Communications Center). A beautiful film that relates the life-giving elements of our daily lives to the celebration of Communion. (2) *Word Is Celebration, Part I* (16mm, color, 30 minutes, produced by CBS). A celebration of Communion with a jazz combo, movement, dancing, clapping, and expressions of joy.

For information on film rentals, see "Movies" in Part Three of this book.

ORDER OF WORSHIP

Begin with an actual meal together. Have everyone (including the worship leader) sit at tables or in a circle on the floor. On the altar or in some other conspicuous place, there should be: cinnamon rolls, Danish pastries, or some other dessert cake (or bread); and lemonade, juice, or some other beverage. When all have finished the meal, begin the Communion service:

Invitation to Communion *(to be said by the worship leader)*
Welcome to this celebration! You are invited to participate in this service of Communion, this Eucharist, this supper of our Lord!
The term "Communion" refers to community. So let us affirm our unity with God and with one another!
The term "Eucharist" means "thanksgiving." So let us be thankful!
The Lord's Supper is the meal by which we remember Jesus our Lord. So let us celebrate his life and the gift of new life that he brings to us!

Hymn: "Let Us Break Bread Together"

Prayer of Confession *(unison)*

O God, forgive us for our failure to follow you completely. We want to be sensitive to the sufferings of others, but we realize that we are often too wrapped up in our own concerns. We want to think loving thoughts, to speak caring words, to act in the spirit of Christ. Yet we often harbor grudges, lash out with angry words, and act in ways that hurt and destroy.

Remind us of our mandate to meet the demands of your gospel. Challenge us with your life-changing message. Forgive us and accept us—so that we may find new life and a new life-style, through Jesus Christ our Lord. Amen.

Words of Hope and Forgiveness: 1 John 1:9 *(to be said by the worship leader)*

Offering and Doxology

Probe of the Word: Sharing of the Communion Elements

Read 1 Corinthians 11:23-25. Then go around the room and give each person a pastry (or piece of cake or bread) and a glass of the beverage. As you serve each person, say: *(name), this represents* (or: *is*) *the body and blood of Jesus our Lord, who gave his life so that you might have forgiveness for your sins and find a new and exciting way of life!* As an alternative, serve everyone and then have each person serve the person on his or her right while saying these or similar words. After all have been served, say: *In a spirit of thankfulness and unity, let us remember our Lord Jesus as we eat and drink together!* Then have everyone take Communion at the same time.

The Lord's Prayer *(unison)*

Hymn: "Bread of the World"

Passing of the Peace: Have everyone pass the peace by shaking hands with the person on his or her right and saying: *(name), may God's peace go with you!*

WORSHIP SERVICE NO. 5: "COMMUNICATING WITH ONE ANOTHER"

Guidelines for the Basic Service

Purpose: To give persons an opportunity to learn some communication skills in a worship service.

Resources and Materials Needed: Bibles, hymnals; headbands (see instructions below)

Hymns. The two suggested hymns are found in many hymnals. Alternative ideas are given in "Additional Ideas for This Service."

Offering and Doxology. This section is optional. For ideas on Doxologies, see "Additional Hymns and Service Music" in Part Three of this book.

Scripture. Mark 9:30-37 relates an incident when Jesus' disciples failed to respond to his attempts to tell them of his anxieties about his impending death. The disciples are too concerned about their own ambitions and plans to listen openly to what Jesus is saying. Before reading this selection in the service, point out that it is a classic example of how communication is blocked by the failure to listen empathetically. James 1:19 urges Christians to give preference to listening rather than speaking and to avoid anger. The TEV is preferred for both readings.

Probe of the Word. This part of the service is designed to give participants an opportunity to experience both poor communication and good communication. In preparation for the first part of this probe, you will need to make special headbands (one for each person). Make the headbands as shown in the illustration and write one of the following statements on each headband (you may use any statement more than one time); "Agree with everything I say." "Laugh when I talk." "Act *very* interested in what I am saying." "Disagree with everything I say." "Interrupt me when I talk." "Look away from me when I talk." "Change the subject when I talk." "Ignore me when I talk."

STRIP (APPROXIMATELY 2" x 5"
CUT FROM LARGE INDEX CARDS

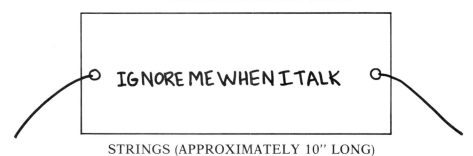

STRINGS (APPROXIMATELY 10" LONG)

Additional Ideas for This Service

If you have additional time and/or resources, you may wish to consider some of the following suggestions for alteration of the basic service:

Hymns. For the *first* hymn, substitute the standard hymn "Love Divine, All Loves Excelling." For the *second* hymn, substitute the standard hymn "Christ, From Whom All Blessings Flow" or one of these folk hymns: "There's a Quiet Understanding" (*Exodus Songbook*); "Listen" (*Listen*); "Tear Down the Walls" (in "Additional Hymns and Service Music" in Part Three of this book).

Movies. You may wish to use one of these movies about communication skills: (1) *Miscommunications* (16mm, color, 5 minutes, produced by John Taylor). A humorous animated film that teaches four communication skills. (2) *Transactions; Feelings* (16mm, color, 30 minutes each, produced by United Methodist Communications). Two of the films in the *Learning to Live* series, which deals with transactional analysis. For information on film rentals, see "Movies" in Part Three of this book.

ORDER OF WORSHIP

Call to Worship *(responsively)*
God is speaking to us, but sometimes we fail to hear God's words.
We will listen for God's voice.
When other people speak to us, we sometimes do not really hear them.
We will try to listen to one another.
Let us be open to God and to one another as we worship together.

Hymn: "Jesus, Lord, We Look to Thee"

Prayer of Reflection *(unison)*

O God, help us to open our ears and our hearts to you and to one another. Make us aware of the feelings and the fears that are so often buried beneath the spoken words. Make us sensitive to the sorrows that are masked by smiles and the needs that are disguised by gestures. Help us to hear what is really being said and not just what we want to hear. Help us to listen so that we may sense what is hidden in other people's hearts. Strengthen us so that we may be able to love others in the way that you have taught us. Amen.

Offering and Doxology

Scripture: Mark 9:30-37; James 1:19

Probe of the Word: Learning to Communicate

Tie one of the headbands onto each participant without letting that person see what is written on the headband. Then give the whole group a subject to discuss (for example: Why my school is the best one around). Tell the participants that they must follow the headband instructions during the discussion. Continue the discussion until every person guesses what is on his or her headband or until a pre-set time period has elapsed. Afterward, talk about the effect of the headband instructions on the discussion. Give particular emphasis to the ways in which we "pigeon-hole" persons (for example, considering some people's opinions very valuable and other people's opinions worthless).

For the second part of the probe, have three persons sit in front of the group and discuss another topic (for example: How can this youth group be improved?). Two of the persons are to carry on the actual discussion. The third person by pointing out to each of the other two the instances when communication is blocked by not listening, not responding to questions, ignoring remarks, and so forth. Afterward, discuss with the whole group the communication skills learned in this activity.

Conclude the probe by discussing how the two activities relate to the Scripture passages used in the service.

Hymn: "God Be With You 'Til We Meet Again"

Benediction *(to be said by the worship leader)*
Go forth to listen, to learn, to love. Go forth in openness to other people so that you may discover how to care for others as Jesus did. Amen.

WORSHIP SERVICE NO. 6: "THE REAL WAY"

Guidelines for the Basic Service

Purpose: To give persons an opportunity to examine the direction of their lives in a worship service.

Resources and Materials Needed: Bibles, hymnals; pencils and pieces of paper

Hymns. The two suggested hymns are found in many hymnals. Alternative ideas are given in "Additional Ideas for This Service."

Offering and Doxology. This section is optional. For ideas on Doxologies, see "Additional Hymns and Service Music" in Part Three of this book.

Scripture. Psalms 1 describes two ways of life: the way of the righteous person and the way of the unrighteous person. The RSV is recommended. Psalms 139:23-24 is part of a prayer in which the writer asks to be guided in "the everlasting way." The TEV is preferred. In Matthew 7:13-14, Jesus contrasts the easy way of the sinner's life with the more difficult path of those who follow him. Again, the TEV is preferred. John 14:6 is Jesus' famous statement: "I am the way, and the truth, and the life."

Probe of the Word. This part of the service is designed to give participants an opportunity to examine their lives from past and future perspectives. The main activity consists of the creation of "life-maps." An example is given in the illustration below.

A SAMPLE LIFE MAP

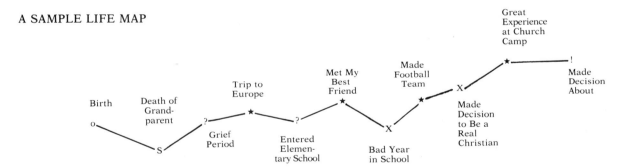

Additional Ideas for This Service

If you have additional time and/or resources, you may wish to consider some of the following suggestions for alteration of the basic service:

Hymns. Substitute standard hymns or folk hymns for those suggested in the basic service. Alternatives for the *first* hymn: (1) *Standard Hymns:* "Guide Me, O Thou Great Jehovan"; "Now Thank We All Our God"; (2) *Folk Hymn:* "You Are the Way" (*A New Commandment*).

Alternatives for the *second* hymn: (1) *Standard Hymns:* "Take My Life and Let It Be Consecrated"; "All the Way My Savior Leads Me"; "When We Walk With the Lord" ("Trust and Obey"); "Walk in the Light"; (2) *Folk Hymns:* "It's a Long Road to Freedom" (*Joy Is Like the Rain*); "All Along the Way" (*Listen*); "On Our Way" (*Exodus Songbook*); "Day by Day"; "Just a Closer Walk With Thee" (both in *The Genesis Songbook*).

Movies. You may wish to show one of the following movies dealing with the Christian way of life: (1) *Beginning Now* (16mm, color, 5 minutes, produced by United Methodist Communications). An allegorical film about a group of people waiting in a clearing for "it" (God's grace? the Kingdom? the Way of Life?) to appear. (2) *Parable* (16mm, color, 22 minutes, produced by Rolf Forsburg). A classic film about a clown, a Christ-figure whom some people follow and others persecute. For information on film rentals, see "Movies" in Part Three of this book.

ORDER OF WORSHIP

Call to Worship *(to be said by the worship leader)*

Jesus said: "I am the way, and the truth, and the life." Let us worship our God, who through Jesus showed us the true way to live.

Hymn: "God of the Ages, by Whose Hand"

Prayer of Reflection *(unison)*

O God, you walk beside us in our lives. You are our companion on the journey. You are always with us —even when we do not recognize your presence.

Pause with us in this moment of prayer. Refresh us with your life-giving spirit. Comfort us with your word. Reveal to us our part and our present, so that we may be strengthened to face our future.

Lay our lives out before us. Give us a realistic view of who we are and a compelling vision of what we might become—through Jesus Christ who leads us along the road to life and joy. Amen.

Scripture from the Old Testament: Psalms 1; Psalms 139:23-24

Offering and Doxology

Scripture from the New Testament: Matthew 7:13-14; John 14:6

Probe of the Word: Finding Our Way

Hand out pencils and pieces of paper. Give directions for making "life maps"; then have each person spend a few minutes making a "life map" to show the course of his or her life up to this point. Directions are as follows: Ascending lines show movement toward high points in one's life; descending lines show movement toward low points in one's life. Symbols may be used to indicate crucial points. Here are some examples: o = birth; X = a crisis; S = a time of sadness; ? = a time of uncertainty; ★ = a time of joy or fulfillment; + = a religious experience; ! = a time when an important decision was made. Descriptive phrases may be written in, but these are not necessary. The "Sample Life Map" may be used as an example.

After everyone has completed the activity, have a period of sharing. Then have participants work individually to answer the following questions:

1. What are three important goals that you have for your life?
2. How would you describe your life as you think it will be twenty years from now?
3. In what important way will you make the world a better place because of your life?
4. What epitaph would you write for your tombstone?
5. How will your Christian faith affect the course of your life?

Afterward, share and discuss responses.

Hymn: "O Master, Let Me Walk With Thee"

Benediction *(to be said by the worship leader)*

Go forth to walk in the way of Christ. Live out your life as God's spirit directs you. Amen.

WORSHIP SERVICE NO. 7: "PEACE ON EARTH"
(World Order Sunday)

Guidelines for the Basic Service

Purpose: To sensitize persons to issues of war and peace during a worship service.

Resources and Materials Needed: Bibles, hymnals; pencils and pieces of paper; newsprint and markers; *or* chalkboard, chalk, and eraser.

Hymns. The two suggested hymns are found in many hymnals. Alternative ideas are given in "Additional Ideas for This Service."

Offering and Doxology. This section is optional. For ideas on Doxologies, see "Additional Hymns and Service Music" in Part Three of this book.

Scripture. Isaiah 2:2-4 is one of the Old Testament's most compelling prophecies about an ideal future, in which the world is at peace. Matthew 5:9 is Jesus' Beatitude about peacemakers. The TEV is preferred for both selections.

Probe of the Word. This part of the service consists of a group activity in which persons brainstorm about ways in which ordinary persons can work for world peace. Since many youth are not particularly knowledgeable on this subject, it will probably be necessary for the adult leader to work very closely with the youth on this activity. It is highly recommended that you consider bringing in some *outside resource persons* such as peace activists, members of anti-nuclear groups, pastors, and/or social studies teachers.

Additional Ideas for This Service

If you have additional time and/or resources, you may wish to consider some of the following suggestions for alteration of the basic service:

Hymns. Substitute standard hymns or folk hymns for those suggested in the basic service. Alternatives for the *first* hymn: (1) *Standard Hymns:* "From All That Dwell Below the Skies"; "We've a Story to Tell to the Nations"; (2) *Folk Hymn:* "They'll Know We Are Christians by Our Love" (*Songbook for Saints and Sinners, The Genesis Songbook,* and other collections).

Alternatives for the *second* hymn: (1) *Standard Hymns:* "These Things Shall Be"; "God of Grace and God of Glory"; (2) *Folk Hymns:* "Kyrie, America"; "New World Coming" (both in *Exodus Songbook*); "Down by the Riverside"; "What a Great Thing It Is"; "I'd Like to Teach the World to Sing"; "One Tin Soldier"; "Let There Be Peace on Earth"—change "brothers" to "neighbors" (all in *The Genesis Songbook*).

Movies. You may wish to use one of these movies: (1) *American Time Capsule* (16mm, color, 3 minutes, produced by Pyramid Films). A fast-moving film about America's history—particularly its wars. (2) *The Hat* (16mm, color, 18 minutes, produced by John and Faith Hubley). An animated film about two soldiers from opposing armies who have an encounter with each other. For information on film rentals, see "Movies" in Part Three of this book.

Recorded Music. As a prelude and/or postlude, use one of the anti-war songs of the 1960's and 1970's by singers such as Joan Baez, Bob Dylan, Tom Paxton, Phil Ochs, or Peter, Paul, and Mary. For a more contemporary selection, use one of the songs from Pink Floyd's Columbia album *The Final Cut.*

Game. As an alternative Probe of the Word, use the simulation game "Crunch" from Dennis Benson's book *Gaming* (Nashville: Abingdon, 1971).

An Alternative Prayer of Confession. If you would like to have the prayer of confession expressed musically, have a soloist or a group sing "Kyrie, America" (from *Exodus Songbook*) rather than using this song as a hymn.

ORDER OF WORSHIP

Call to Worship *(responsively)*
  God created the world, and God knew that it was a good creation!
  But human beings have created war, which is an evil creation!
  God continually calls us to restore the goodness of God's creation. God calls us to be peacemakers.
  But we have not taken that call seriously.
  Let us resolve to take God's call seriously. Let us seek out the new creation that is on our horizon. Let us work for a peaceful world as we worship God together.

Hymn: "Break Forth, O Living Light of God"

Prayer of Confession *(unison)*

  O God, you sent the Prince of Peace to show us the path to peace and joy, but we have not followed that path. Instead, we have trudged along on the trails that lead to hatred and discord. We have filled our lives with prejudice and distrust. We have not done all that we could to work for peace in the world. Forgive us our failures, and make us instruments of your peace—so that war may vanish from the face of the earth. Amen.

Offering and Doxology

Scripture: Isaiah 2:2-4; Matthew 5:9

Probe of the Word: How to Be a Peacemaker

  Divide the group into small teams of two or three persons. Give each person a pencil and a piece of paper. Have the teams brainstorm for a few minutes on this question: "What are some actions that I can take to work for peace in the world?" Suggest that each team try to come up with a half dozen or so ideas that are practical and realistic.

  Afterward, have each group report its suggestions. Collate the responses on newsprint or a chalkboard. Discuss the suggestions. Have the group choose at least five actions that are practical—that is, realistic and within the capabilities of group members. Then make some action plans, and spend a few minutes discussing ways in which various persons will carry out the group's plans. Finally, decide on a future date when persons will report their actions to the group.

Prayer for Peace *(to be prayed by the worship leader)*
  O God, give us peace in our time! Deliver us from the violence of war. Help us to avoid the temptation to distrust other nations. Put your compassion in our hearts and your wisdom in our minds, so that we may put our trust in you rather than in the weapons of war. Amen.

Hymn: "O Day of God, Draw Nigh"

Benediction *(to be passed from one person to another as all stand in a circle)*
  Go now in peace, and may God go with you as you work for peace in the world. Amen.

WORSHIP SERVICE NO. 8: "RENEWING THE CHURCH"

Guidelines for the Basic Service

Purpose: To give persons an opportunity to consider church renewal during a worship service.

Resources and Materials Needed: Bibles; hymnals; pencils and pieces of paper.

Hymns. The two suggested hymns are found in many hymnals. Alternative ideas are given in "Additional Ideas for This Service."

Offering and Doxology. This section is optional. For ideas on Doxologies, see "Additional Hymns and Service Music" in Part Three of this book.

Scripture. Deuteronomy 30:15-20 is part of Moses' speech to the people of Israel as they prepare to enter the Promised Land. Moses urges them to be the true people of God by choosing God's way of life and following God's commandments. Matthew 25:31-46 is Jesus' Parable of the Last Judgment, which gives criteria by which the church may measure its effectiveness. The TEV is recommended for both selections.

Probe of the Word. This part of the service consists primarily of a trial of the church (or a trial of a youth group). You will need to read through this material, assign roles (Judge, Prosecutor, and Defense Attorney), and discuss plans for the trial prior to the service. The indictment against the church (or the youth group) should read as follows: "The church (or youth group) is charged with failure to fulfill its mission as taught by Jesus Christ." The cases for the prosecution and for the defense should be prepared in advance.

Additional Ideas for This Service

If you have additional time and/or resources, you may wish to consider some of the following suggestions for alteration of the basic service:

Hymns. Substitute standard hymns or folk hymns for those suggested in the basic service. Alternatives for the *first* hymn: (1) *Standard Hymns:* "The Church's One Foundation"; "Christ Is Made the Sure Foundation"; (2) *Folk Hymn:* "Psalm of Thanksgiving" (*Exodus Songbook*).

Alternatives for the *second* hymn: (1) *Standard Hymns:* "One Holy Church of God Appears"; "I Love Thy Kingdom, Lord"; (2) *Folk Hymns:* "The Church Within Us" (*The Genesis Songbook*); "We Are the Church" (*Songbook for Saints and Sinners*); "God Give His People Strength" (*Joy Is Like the Rain*).

Movies. You may wish to use one of the following movies dealing with the nature and mission of the church: (1) *And Then* (16mm, color, 16 minutes). An unusual film about how church members appear to some young confirmands with *big* Bibles. (2) *Beggar at the Gates* (16mm, color, 56 minutes, produced by Bill Heller). An older film with a timely message about the church's responsibility to be involved in social action ministries. (3) *Church in the World* (16mm, color, 20 minutes, produced by P. K.). A film about how the gospel relates to the needs of the world. (4) *Celebrate Church Alive* (16mm, color, 27 minutes, produced by Pat Bates). A film showing congregations that are relevant to today's world.

For information on film rentals, see "Movies" in Part Three of this book.

ORDER OF WORSHIP

Call to Worship *(responsively)*
Who are you?
We are the people of God! We are the church!
What does it mean to be the church?
It means following the teachings of Jesus Christ. It means loving and caring for people. It means helping people in need.
Then let us worship God and learn how to follow, how to love, how to care.

Hymn: "A Mighty Fortress Is Our God"

Prayer of Reflection *(unison)*

O God, you have given us the church. It should be a community of joy, but it often seems like a collection of sour face and dull voices. It should be inspired by daring dreams, but it often seems to be dragged down by dismal despair. It should be a wellspring of love, but it often seems to be a source of distrust and unconcern.

O God, as we look at the church, help us also to look at ourselves—for we are the church. Show us how to examine ourselves, so that we may become the church that we were meant to be. Amen.

Scripture from the Old Testament: Deuteronomy 30:15-20

Offering and Doxology

Scripture from the New Testament: Matthew 25:31-46

Probe of the Word: The Church on Trial
In preparation for the trial, point out that the church has usually renewed itself through constructive criticisms from persons *within* the church (like Martin Luther, John Wesley, and Pope John XXIII). Then emphasize that this activity is to be a constructive one with a positive purpose.

Have the Judge (or someone acting as Clerk) read the indictment. Then proceed with the trial as outlined below. The Judge is to preside and keep order. You may select persons to serve as a Jury; or the whole group may assume this role.

Order of Trial Proceedings: (1) *The Case for the Prosecution*—presented by the Prosecutor; (2) *The Case for the Defense*—presented by the Defense Attorney; (3) *Recall of Witnesses for the Prosecution*—done by the Prosecutor; (4) *Final Argument for the Defense*—presented by the Defense Attorney; (5) *Final Argument for the Prosecution*—presented by the Prosecutor; (6) *Jury Discussion*; (7) *Verdict.*

After the trial, discuss how what you learned in this activity may help you to improve the church's (or the youth group's) program and ministry.

Hymn: "Jesus, With Thy Church Abide"

Benediction *(to be said by the worship leader)*
Go forth as renewed people! Renew the church and the world! Amen.

WORSHIP SERVICE NO. 9: "SAINTS AMONG US"
(All Saints Day)

Guidelines for the Basic Service

Purpose: To give persons an opportunity to participate in a worship service in which they gain an awareness of the influence of other Christians on their lives.

Resources and Materials Needed: Bibles, hymnals, a pencil and a piece of paper for each participant; offering plate(s) (optional)

Hymns. The two suggested hymns are found in many hymnals. Alternative ideas are given in "Additional Ideas for This Service."

Offering and Doxology. This part of the service will give participants an opportunity to express their thankfulness for Christians who have influenced their lives. For ideas on Doxologies, see "Additional Hymns and Service Music" in Part Three of this book.

Scripture. Revelation 7:9-17 presents a vision of the heavenly blessings that are in store for faithful Christians—those who have demonstrated their "sainthood" by keeping the faith despite hard times. Matthew 5:1-12 is the famous passage known as the Beatitudes—a listing of the qualities and blessings for true Christians.

Probe of the Word. This part of the service is designed to help participants become aware of how they have been helped by persons who are loving, caring Christians. By discussing the influence of these modern-day "saints," the worshipers should become aware of the characteristics of a Christian lifestyle.

Additional Ideas for This Service

If you have additional time and/or resources, you may wish to consider some of the following suggestions for alteration of the basic service:

Hymns. Substitute standard hymns or folk hymns for those suggested in the basic service. Alternatives for the *first* hymn: (1) *Standard Hymns:* "Jesus Where'er Thy People Meet"; "All Praise to Our Redeeming Lord"; (2) *Folk Hymn:* "They'll Know We Are Christians by Our Love" (*Songbook for Saints and Sinners, The Genesis Songbook,* and other collections).

Alternatives for the *second* hymn: (1) *Standard Hymns:* "I Would Be True"; "Come, Let Us Join Our Friends Above"; "Through All the Changing Scenes of Life"; "Blest Be the Tie That Binds." (2) *Folk Hymns:* "Moments to Live By"; "All I Ask of You" (both in *Listen*); "I Believe in You" (*A New Commandment*); "I'll Sing a Song of the Saints of God" (in various sources, including Episcopal hymnals).

Movies. You may wish to show one of the following movies: (1) *Portrait of Grandpa Doc* (16mm, color, 28 minutes, produced by Pyramid Films). A film about a man's influence on his grandson. (2) *Angel and Big Joe* (16mm, color, 27 minutes). A film about the positive effects of a telephone repairman's concern for a young boy.

For information on film rentals, see "Movies" in Part Three of this book.

Solo. Have a soloist sing "Song for a Friend" (in "Additional Hymns and Service Music" in Part Three of this book), "You Are the Salt of the Earth" (*Avery and Marsh Songbook*), or "Wherever You Go" (*Wherever You Go*).

Recorded Music. For a prelude, offertory, or postlude, use James Taylor's recording of Carole King's song "You've Got a Friend" (from his Warner album *Greatest Hits*) and/or Dan Fogelberg's recording of his song "Leader of the Band" (from his Full Moon/Epic album *The Innocent Age*).

Poster. Make and display a poster using the free-verse poem included in the song "Wherever You Go" (in the songbook *Wherever You Go*).

ORDER OF WORSHIP

Call to Worship *(responsively)*
God loves you! I love you! Many other people love you!
We are truly blessed by God's love and by the love of our families and friends!
Let us worship God and give thanks for all the love that surrounds us.

Hymn: "For All the Saints"

Prayer of Reflection *(unison)*
O God, we are aware of the ways in which you use other people to express your love for us. Loving and caring people have nurtured us in our times of need. They have molded our minds. They have been a light for our lives. They have eased our pain and shared our joys.

Give us insight and strength so that we, too, may become friends and helpers for those who need us. Help us to be like our best friend, Jesus the Christ. Amen.

Scripture: Revelation 7:9-17; Matthew 5:1-12

Probe of the Word: Saints Among Us
Give each person a pencil and a piece of paper. Have each person spend a few minutes writing the names of three persons who have had a significant positive influence on his or her life and ways in which that influence was expressed.

Afterward, have a period of sharing. Have each person in turn report on at least one person's influence on his or her life. After each person has finished sharing, have the entire group respond with this litany:

O God, we thank you for the way in which____ (name)____ has influenced the life of our friend _____ (name)____ .

After everyone has had an opportunity to share with the group, discuss the activity. Sample discussion questions: "What caused these persons to be so helpful to you? Were these persons' actions influenced by their faith? If so, how? In what ways can you express your gratitude for these persons' actions? In what ways can these persons' actions serve as a model for your life?"

After the discussion, have participants fold their sheets of paper prior to putting them in the offering plate or on the altar. If your group takes an offering during its meeting, offerings of money may also be given at this time.

Offering and Doxology

Prayer of Dedication *(unison)*
O God, accept these offerings as our expression of our gratitude for the good lives that you have given to us. We thank you especially for those persons who have shared their love and your love with us. Help us to give of ourselves so that we may pass that love on to others. Amen.

Hymn: "Jesus, Lord, We Look to Thee"

Benediction *(to be said by the worship leader)*
Go forth to share the love that has been shared with you. Amen.

WORSHIP SERVICE NO. 10: "OVERCOMING OUR DIFFERENCES"

Guidelines for the Basic Service

Purpose: To give persons an opportunity to participate in a worship service in which they learn about overcoming differences among people.

Resources and Materials Needed: Bibles; hymnals; collage materials; old magazines, poster board, glue, scissors, felt-tipped markers; pencils and paper.

Hymns. The two suggested hymns are found in many hymnals. Alternative ideas are given in "Additional Ideas for This Service."

Offering and Doxology. This section is optional. For ideas on Doxologies, see "Additional Hymns and Service Music" in Part Three of this book.

Scripture. Ephesians 4:1-6 is a statement about the unity of the church. Colossians 3:8-11 teaches that we should not make distinctions among people but rather accept all people in the spirit of Christ. The RSV is preferred for the first selection, and the TEV is preferred for the second.

Probe of the Word. This part of the service is designed to help participants: (1) understand their feelings about persons who are "different" from them; and (2) work to change those feelings that are negative.

In preparation for this probe, you will need to make a collage as follows: Cut from old magazines twenty pictures of person's faces. Make sure that you have a variety of types—youth and adults of various ages; persons from various ethnic and racial backgrounds; males and females; persons of varying degrees of attractiveness; and so forth. Paste the pictures onto a piece of poster board and number them 1 through 20.

Additional Ideas for This Service

If you have additional time and/or resources, you may wish to consider some of the following suggestions for alteration of the basic service:

Hymns. Substitute standard hymns or folk hymns for those suggested in the basic service. Alternatives for the *first* hymn: (1) *Standard Hymns:* "All People That on Earth Do Dwell"; "In Christ There Is No East or West"; (2) *Folk Hymns:* "They'll Know We Are Christians by Our Love" (*Songbook for Saints and Sinners, The Genesis Songbook,* and other collections); "What a Great Thing It Is" (*The Genesis Songbook*).

Alternatives for the *second* hymn: (1) *Standard Hymns:* "Love Divine, All Loves Excelling"; "Blest Be the Dear Uniting Love"; (2) *Folk Hymns:* "Tear Down the Walls" (in "Additional Hymns and Service Music" in Part Three of this book); "Love One Another"; "I'm OK, You're OK" (both in *Exodus Songbook*); "Sing Love Songs" (*Avery and Marsh Songbook*); "Moments to Live By" (*Listen*).

Movies. You may wish to use one of the following movies: (1) *How's Your New Friend?* (16mm, color, 12 minutes, produced by CRM). A film about a high school clique's reaction to a new girl in school. (2) *Bill Cosby on Prejudice* (16mm, color, 24 minutes, produced by Pyramid Films). A tongue-in-cheek film—a satire on a bigot's tirades against all kinds of people. (3) *The Shopping Bag Lady* (16mm, color, 21 minutes, produced by LCA). A film about a young girl's discovery of the true personality of a street person, an old "shopping bag lady."

For information on film rentals, see "Movies" in Part Three of this book.

ORDER OF WORSHIP

Call to Worship *(responsively)*
People come in all different shapes, sizes, colors, personalities!
And God loves and accepts us all!
Let us worship God together so that we, too, may learn how to love and accept all people.

Hymn: "From All That Dwell Below the Skies"

Prayer of Reflection *(unison)*
O God, we know that you have created every person as a unique, special individual. We are aware of our differences, and we want to celebrate our differences—for they make life interesting and exciting.

Sometimes, however, we are hampered by our differences. They divide us and make us distrust one another. They produce hurt and hatred.

Help us to overcome our differences. Show us the ways in which we are alike. Make us aware of the unity that could exist among all members of the human family, through Jesus Christ who unites us all. Amen.

Scripture: Ephesians 4:1-6; Colossians 3:8-11

Offering and Doxology

Probe of the Word: Learning How to Overcome Our Differences
Have all members of the group look at the collage. Then hand out pencils and pieces of paper and have persons work individually to answer the following questions:

- *If you could choose three of these persons to be your close friends, which ones would you choose?*
- *Which one of these persons would you consider the dumbest?*
- *Which one of these persons would you consider the smartest?*
- *If you could choose one of these persons to accompany you on a trip around the world, which one would you choose?*
- *Which one of these persons would you distrust the most?*
- *Which one of these persons would you trust the most?*

After everyone has finished, share and discuss responses. Have persons give reasons for their choices. Consider what the responses reveal about the participants' attitudes toward people who are similar to them and people who are different from them.

Conclude by discussing ways in which one can overcome prejudices toward people who seem "different." Emphasize the Christian faith's teachings about accepting and caring for all people.

Hymn: "Jesus, Lord, We Look to Thee"

Benediction *(to be said by the worship leader)*
Go out from this place to help create a world of love and acceptance! Help the needy. Care for the lonely. Liberate those who are oppressed. Love and accept every person—just as God loves and accepts you. Amen.

WORSHIP SERVICE NO. 11: "THANKS BE TO GOD!"
(Thanksgiving Sunday)

Guidelines for the Basic Service

Purpose: To give persons an opportunity to express their gratitude to God in a worship service.

Resources and Materials Needed: Bibles; hymnals; a pencil and a piece of paper for each participant; offering plate(s) (optional)

Hymns. The two suggested hymns are found in many hymnals. Alternative ideas are given in "Additional Ideas for This Service."

Offering and Doxology. This section is optional, but it is preferable that it be included, since an offering and a hymn of praise such as the Doxology should ordinarily be a part of a service of thanksgiving.

Scripture. Psalms 100 is a psalm of thanksgiving. First Thessalonians 3:7-9 is one of Paul's many expressions of gratitude to God for the support and encouragement given to Paul by other Christians. The TEV is preferred for both passages.

Probe of the Word. This part of the service is designed to give worshipers an opportunity to express their thankfulness for God's gifts to them.

Additional Ideas for This Service

If you have additional time and/or resources, you may wish to consider some of the following suggestions for alteration of the basic service.

Hymns. Substitute standard hymns and/or folk hymns for those suggested in the basic service. Alternatives for the *first* hymn: (2) *Standard Hymns:* "We, Thy People, Praise Thee"; "We Gather Together"; (2) *Folk Hymns:* "Psalm of Thanksgiving" (*Exodus Songbook*); "Morning Has Broken" (*The Genesis Songbook*).

Alternatives for the *second* hymn: (2) *Standard Hymns:* "My God, I Thank Thee"; "O Lord of Heaven and Earth and Sky"; (2) *Folk Hymns:* "Thank You, Lord"; "Thanks Be to God" (*Songbook for Saints and Sinners*)—may be sung also to the tune of the old song "Windy" by the group The Association.

Solo. Have a soloist sing "All Good Gifts" from the musical *Godspell* (New York: Valando Music, 1971) or "Explorer" (*Avery and Marsh Songbook*).

Slide-and-Tape Presentations. Use slides showing things that persons are thankful for with the recording of "All Good Gifts" (from the Bell Records album of *Godspell*). As an alternative presentation, have someone sing the song "Explorer," while appropriate slides are shown. See the suggestions in the small lead-sheet edition of *Avery and Marsh Songbook* for ideas. For suggestions on making home-made slides, consult the resources on slide-making listed in the "Media" section in Part Three of this book. For ideas on slide-making and slide-and-tape presentations, see pages 116-126 of the C-4 Resources book *Youth Workers' Handbook*, by Steve Clapp and Jerry O. Cook.

Movies. You may wish to use one of the following movies: (1) *From Whom All Blessings Flow* (16mm, color, 12 minutes, produced by United Presbyterian Church, USA). A film showing five Christians who give offerings in church and give of themselves in their daily lives. (2) *The Gift* (16mm, color, 23 minutes, produced by the National Council of Churches). A survey of our Christian heritage that challenges viewers to respond to God's gift of Christ.

For information on film rentals, see "Movies" in Part Three of this book.

ORDER OF WORSHIP

Call to Worship (*responsively*)
This is the day that God has made!
We are thankful for this day and for all of our days!
Let us worship God together. Let us praise God and give thanks.

Hymn: "Now Thank We All Our God"

Prayer of Reflection (*unison*)
O God, sometimes we forget to say "thank you." We accept our blessings, but we don't consider their source. We take and take, but we don't express our appreciation.
Slow us down, O God. Help us to pause and ponder. Make us aware of what we owe to you and to our families and friends. Make us truly thankful, and show us how to say "thank you." Open our hearts and minds, so that we may grow in grace and gratitude, through Jesus Christ our Lord. Amen.

Scripture: Psalms 100; 1 Thessalonians 3:7-9

Probe of the Word: Expressing Gratitude to God
Hand out pencils and pieces of paper. Have each person work individually to write under each of the following categories at least three things for which he or she is thankful: (1) *Talents, Abilities, and Other Personal Characteristics;* (2) *Material Possessions;* (3) *People Who Have Had a Positive Influence on My Life.*
After everyone has finished, have a period of sharing. Go around the group and have each person share his or her responses with the group. After each person has shared, have the group respond with the following litany:

O God, we join with _____ (name) _____ in thanking you for the blessings that you have given. Amen.

Conclude with a discussion of how participants can express their gratitude by "passing on their blessings." Give special emphasis to ways in which participants can help other people and ways in which they can give of themselves in service to God in the church.
In preparation for the offering, have participants fold their sheets—which will be put in the offering plate or on the altar. If your group takes an offering during its meeting, offerings of money may also be given at this time.

Offering and Doxology

Prayer of Dedication (*unison*)
O God, accept these offerings as our written expressions of our gratitude. Make us more aware of our gifts, and help us to share ourselves and our possessions with those who are less fortunate. Amen.

Hymn: "For All the Blessings of the Year"

Benediction (*to be said by the worship leader*)
Go forth from this place to be thankful and sharing people! Amen.

WORSHIP SERVICE NO. 12: "GREAT EXPECTATIONS"
(Christmas Season)

Guidelines for the Basic Service

Purpose: To enable persons to discover in worship a sense of expectation about the coming of Jesus into their lives.

Resources and Materials Needed: Bibles; hymnals; a pencil and a piece of paper for each participant.

Hymns. The two suggested hymns are found in many hymnals. Alternative ideas are given in "Additional Ideas for This Service."

Offering and Doxology. This section is optional. For ideas on Doxologies, see "Additional Hymns and Service Music" in Part Three of this book.

Scripture. Isaiah 11:1-10 presents a prophecy of the coming Messiah that describes the kind of person he will be. This prophecy gives us a portrait of Jesus. Mark 1:1-8 tells of the ministry of John the Baptist and presents his prophetic words about Jesus.

Probe of the Word. This part of the service is designed to help participants get into a mood of expectation and anticipation. You should make sure that everyone is able to transfer feelings concerning his or her own plans to the Christmas season. You may find it helpful in this regard to have a brief discussion about Christmas plans before proceeding to the period of meditation.

Additional Ideas for This Service

If you have additional time and/or resources, you may wish to consider some of the following suggestions for alteration of the basic service:

Hymns. Substitute standard hymns or folk hymns for those suggested in the basic service. *Standard Hymns:* Any of the hymns contained in the Advent section of your hymnal. *Folk Hymns:* "Advent Carol"; "Advent Proclamation"; "When You Least Expect Him" (all in *Avery and Marsh Songbook*); "Wonderful"; "Take Courage" (both in *Gold, Incense and Myrrh*); "Locusts and Wild Honey" (*Locusts and Wild Honey*).

A Musical Call to Worship. Use the song "Prepare Ye (The Way of the Lord)" from the musical *Godspell* a call to worship. The recording is on the Bell album of the musical; the music is published by Valando Music (1971, 1972). Have everyone sing, clap, and dance. If you do the song "live," you may want to use a soloist on the first eight measures of the music.

A Shofar. Borrow a shofar (temple horn) from a synagogue or make one from an animal horn—or use a trumpet or a bugle. Have someone sound the shofar at the beginning of the service. Particularly effective with "Prepare Ye"!

Advent Wreath. Make an Advent wreath. Light the first candle during this service and then light an additional candle each week of Advent. Light the Christ Candle on Christmas Day. (An Advent wreath has five candles — one for each week of Advent and the final one for Christmas day or Christmas Sunday. See the C-4 Resources publication *Shalom: Hope for the World* for more background.)

Movie. Show the movie *The Coming of the Stranger* (16mm, color, 27 minutes, produced by TRAFCO), which is an allegorical telling of the Advent story.

For information on film rentals, see "Movies" in Part Three of this book.

ORDER OF WORSHIP

Call to Worship *(responsively)*
We gather in preparation.
We are prepared to hear good news about our lives.
We gather in expectation.
We expect to find happiness and joy.
We gather in celebration.
We celebrate the promise of hope, peace, and joy.
In preparation, in expectation, in celebration—
Let us worship the God who once again comes into our lives!

Hymn: "O Come, O Come, Emmanuel"

Prayer of Reflection *(unison)*

O God, today we begin again the journey that leads to a barn in Bethlehem. We are excited about the journey and this season. We pray that you will guide us on our journey so that we may press forward to our destination and not be distracted by side roads and bypaths.

All around us we see the neon lights and the brightly-lighted trees. Help us to see beyond them to the one who is the light of the world. All around us we hear the clever advertisements and the jangle of cash registers. Help us to hear above them the sound of the baby Jesus' cry. All around us are the smells and tastes of the season's delicious goodies. Help us to find beyond them the one who is the bread of life.

Direct our eyes and our ears, our minds and our lives toward the Lord who brought love into the world on that first Christmas, and show us how to love as he did. Amen.

Scripture: Isaiah 11:1-10; Mark 1:1-8

Offering and Doxology

Probe of the Word: Great Expectations
Hand out pencils and paper. Have each person take a few minutes to respond to the following statements: *(1) Name one good thing that you expect to happen in your life next week. (2) Name one good thing that you expect to happen in your life during the coming year. (3) Name one good thing that you expect to happen in your life during the next ten years.* Then go around the room and ask each person to share his or her response to each statement. Deal with each statement separately.

Afterward, point out that the sense of expectation that group members feel about their lives is the kind of feeling that Christians have traditionally felt before Christmas. Then ask everyone to meditate in silence a few moments about how they will observe Christmas this year and how the spirit of Jesus might affect their lives during this season.

Hymn: "Come, Thou Long-Expected Jesus"

Benediction *(to be said by the worship leader)*
Go into the world in peace! May the Lord fulfill your expectations! Amen.

WORSHIP SERVICE NO. 13: "GIVING GOOD GIFTS"
(Christmas Season)

Guidelines for the Basic Service

Purpose: To give persons an opportunity to participate in a worship service in which they learn about responsible gift-giving.

Resources and Materials Needed: Bibles; hymnals; pencils and pieces of paper

Hymns. The two suggested hymns are found in many hymnals. Alternative ideas are given in "Additional Ideas for This Service."

Offering and Doxology. This section is optional. For ideas on Doxologies, see "Additional Hymns and Service Music" in Part Three of this book.

Scripture. Isaiah 52:13-53:5 is part of the famous "Suffering Servant" passage, in which Isaiah proclaims the coming of a Messiah who will be humble and ordinary-looking—in sharp contrast to the conventional expectation of a strong and powerful military leader. In Matthew 7:9-12, Jesus points out that God gives good and useful gifts to people and suggests that a prudent person acts in a similar manner. Philippians 2:5-9 is the famous "kenosis" (Greek for "emptying") passage in which Paul describes Jesus as one who gave up power and acclaim in order to follow a simple and humble way.

Probe of the Word. This part of the service is designed to help worshipers examine their attitudes about Christmas gift-giving and develop more responsible attitudes.

Additional Ideas for This Service

If you have additional time and/or resources, you may wish to consider some of the following suggestions for alteration of the basic service:

Hymns. Substitute standard hymns or folk hymns for the hymns suggested in the basic service. Alternatives for the *first* hymn: (1) *Standard Hymns:* Any of the hymns in the Advent section of your hymnal. (2) *Folk Hymns:* "Advent Carol"; "Advent Proclamation"; "When You Least Expect Him"; "Here We Go A-Caroling" (all in *Avery and Marsh Songbook*); "Wonderful"; "Take Courage" (both in *Gold, Incense and Myrrh*); "Locusts and Wild Honey" (*Locusts and Wild Honey*).

Alternatives for the *second* hymn: (1) *Standard Hymns:* "Take My Life and Let It Be Consecrated"; "Lord, Speak to Me"; "In the Bleak Midwinter." (2) *Folk Hymns:* "Thank You, Lord" (*Avery and Marsh Songbook*); "Song for a Friend" (in "Additional Hymns and Service Music" in Part Three of this book; "Pass It On" (in the musical *Tell It Like It Is*—Lexicon Music, 1960; also in many songbooks).

Advent Wreath. Light the first and second candles during the service.

Movies. You may wish to use one of the following movies: (1) *A Clown Is Born* (16mm, color, 15 minutes, produced by Faith and Fantasy, Inc.). A wordless parable about how a clown finds fulfillment in helping a down-and-out hobo. (2) *Christmas Bus* (16mm, color, 20 minutes, produced by Family Films). A film about how people on a city bus discover the true meaning of Christmas when they relate to one another.

For information on film rentals, see "Movies" in Part Three of this book.

Resource. For additional ideas on alternative celebrations see the C-4 Resources book *Repairing Christian Lifestyles.*

ORDER OF WORSHIP

Call to Worship *(responsively)*
It is a season of preparation!
It is the time when we look forward to Christmas!
During this time of year we celebrate God's gift of Jesus the Christ.
What can we do to celebrate this gift?
Let us worship God together, so that we might learn how to celebrate and how to give good gifts.

Hymn: "Lift Up Your Heads, Ye Mighty Gates"

Prayer of Confession *(unison)*

O God, you are the giver of all good gifts. In Jesus the Christ, you have given us the greatest gift in the world.

We confess that we have not always been responsible in our gift-giving. We have been led astray by the lure of money. We have tried to out-do one another by giving expensive presents. We have wasted our money on material things. And we have failed to give of ourselves in love.

Forgive us for our errors. Fill us with Christ-like love, so that we may be more responsible in giving to one another. Amen.

Words of Forgiveness and Hope *(to be said by the worship leader)*
You are forgiven. You are accepted. You are loved. Give yourselves in love as you celebrate this holy season.

Scripture from the Old Testament: Isaiah 52:13-53:5

Offering and Doxology

Scripture from the New Testament: Matthew 7:9-12; Philippians 2:5-9

Probe of the Word: Responsible Gift-giving
Discuss alternative gift-giving. Decide on some action plans. You may use your own ideas or some of the following suggestions: (1) Give personally-written letters of appreciation to persons who have been helpful to you. (2) Give a service organization a donation in someone's honor. (3) Give friends and/or relatives letters in which you promise to do particular things for them. (4) Buy some of your gifts from a shop or organization that uses its profits for service purposes. (5) Give some home-made gifts. (6) Don't send Christmas cards. If you do choose to send cards, buy them from a service organization such as UNICEF or reuse cards that you received last year and donate the money you save to charity. (7) Wrap gifts in comic pages rather than using store bought wrapping paper. (8) Give a used item (a book, a record, or other reusable item). (9) Give gifts to needy children. (10) Give home-made Christmas decorations.

Hymn: "We Give Thee But Thine Own"

Benediction *(to be said by the worship leader)*
Go forth in the spirit of Christ. Be responsible as you give your gifts. Amen.

WORSHIP SERVICE NO. 14: "GETTING OURSELVES READY"
(Christmas Season)

Guidelines for the Basic Service

Purpose: To give persons an opportunity to participate in a worship service in which they examine themselves in preparation for Christmas.

Resources and Materials Needed: Bibles; hymnals; pencils and pieces of paper; waste can; offering plate(s) (optional)

Hymns. The two suggested hymns are found in many hymnals. Alternative ideas are given in "Additional Ideas for This Service."

Offering and Doxology. This section is optional. For ideas on Doxologies, see "Additional Hymns and Service Music" in Part Three of this book.

Scripture. Malachi 3:1-7*b* is a call to repentance. It include God's promise to accept those who turn back to God. Mark 13:33-37 admonishes people to watch and to be prepared for the coming of the Messiah.

Probe of the Word. This part of the service is designed to help participants prepare themselves for Christmas. This call for preparation echoes a theme from the early church, which viewed Advent as being, like Lent, a time of penitence and preparation.

Additional Ideas for This Service

If you have additional time and/or resources, you may wish to consider some of the following suggestions for alteration of the basic service:

Hymns. Substitute standard hymns or folk hymns for those suggested in the basic service. Alternatives for the *first* hymn: (1) *Standard Hymns:* Any hymns in the Advent section of your hymnal. (2) *Folk Hymns:* "Advent Carol"; "Advent Proclamation"; "When You Least Expect Him"; "Here We Go A-Caroling" (all in *Avery and Marsh Songbook*); "Wonderful"; "Take Courage" (both in *Gold, Incense and Myrrh*); "Locusts and Wild Honey"—change "Man" in refrain to "We" (*Locusts and Wild Honey*).

Alternatives for the *second* hymn: (1) *Standard Hymns:* "Just As I Am, Thine Own to Be"; "O Master, Let Me Walk With Thee." (2) *Folk Hymn:* "With What Great Love" (*Abba, Father*).

Advent Wreath. Light the first, second, and third candles during the service.

Solo. Have a soloist sing "Somewhere" or "A Simple Song" (both in *Exodus Songbook*).

An Audio-visual Call to Confession. Use the song "Desperado" as the musical component of an audio-visual call to confession. You may choose to use either the original recording by the Eagles on their Asylum album *Greatest Hits (Volume I)* or Linda Ronstadt's recording on her album.

While the recording is playing, show slides depicting wasteful affluence and scenes related to harmful indulgences (drugs, alcohol, tobacco, and so forth). For suggestions on making home-made slides, consult the resources on slide-making listed in the "Media" section in Part Three of this book. For ideas on slide-making and slide-and-tape presentations, see pages 116-126 of the C-4 Resources book *Youth Workers' Handbook*, by Steve Clapp and Jerry O. Cook.

Movie. You may wish to use the movie *Beginning Now* (16mm, color, 5 minutes, produced by United Methodist Communications), which depicts people waiting in a clearing for "it" (revelation? the Kingdom of God?) to appear in their lives.

For information on film rentals, see "Movies" in Part Three of this book.

ORDER OF WORSHIP

Call to Worship *(responsively)*
It is a season of expectation!
It is a time of preparation for Christmas!
Let us worship God together as we prepare ourselves.

Hymn: "Lord Christ, When First Thou Cam'st"

Prayer of Confession *(unison)*

O God, we need to get ourselves ready for the celebration of the birth of Jesus. We have done many things that we should not have done, and we have failed to do many things that we should have done. We stand in need of your forgiveness and your acceptance.

Show us the sacrifices that we should make. Show us how to celebrate this season of joy and wonder. Forgive us our sins, and prepare us for the coming of your Son and our Lord. Amen.

Words of Forgiveness and Hope *(to be said by the worship leader)*
God forgives you and accepts you! Face the future with hope in your hearts and joy in your lives!

Scripture: Malachi 3:1-7b; Mark 13:33-37

Probe of the Word: Preparation for Christmas
Give each person a pencil and two pieces of paper. Have persons work individually to write at least one response in each of the following categories:

1. Way(s) in Which I Have Sinned by Hurting Another Person (or Other Persons)
2. Habit(s) and/or Thing(s) That I Will Give Up Between Now and Christmas
3. Some Thing(s) I Will Do to Help Someone Else During This Season

The responses in the first two categories should be written on the first sheet of paper and the response in the third category should be written on the second sheet.

After all have finished, have a period of voluntary sharing. Since these responses could be very personal, no one should be pressured to share aloud.

When all who wish to share have had a chance to do so, have everyone come to the front of the room, tear his or her first sheet into shreds, and drop it into the waste can. Then have the group respond with this litany: *O God, as we destroy these sheets of paper, we ask that you will blot out the offenses that we have written. Forgive us for our shortcomings, and give us new life—through Jesus Christ our Lord. Amen.*

Have participants fold the other sheets and place them—along with any offerings of money—in the offering plate(s) or on the altar during the offering.

Offering and Doxology

Hymn: "Lord, I Want to Be a Christian"

Benediction *(to be said by the worship leader)*
Go forth as forgiven people! Prepare for the birth of the Christ!

WORSHIP SERVICE NO. 15: "SYMBOLS OF THE FAITH"
(Christmas Season)

Guidelines for the Basic Service

Purpose: To give persons an opportunity to participate in a worship service in which they become more aware of some symbols related to Jesus and his ministry.

Resources and Materials Needed: Bibles; hymnals; a Christmas tree (a cedar or other evergreen); materials for decorations: cardboard, aluminum foil, glue or tape; string; scissors

Hymns. The two suggested hymns are found in many hymnals. Alternative ideas are given in "Additional Ideas for This Service."

Offering and Doxology. This section is optional. For ideas on Doxologies, see "Additional Hymns and Service Music" in Part Three of this book.

Scripture. Isaiah 62:10-12 is a prophecy of the gift of salvation that the Messiah will bring to God's people—symbolized here by the city of Jerusalem. Deuteronomy 6:4-9 includes the famous Shema (Hebrew for "Hear" or "Remember"—a reference to the first word of the Shema, verses 4-5). This selection also includes the admonition to write God's commandments on doorposts (mezuzahs) and on phylacteries to be worn on foreheads and arms. This selection is thus one of the earliest Biblical passages relating to symbolic memory aids. The TEV is preferred for both selections.

Probe of the Word. This part of the service is designed to help worshipers become more aware of symbols related to the life of Jesus. The main activity consists of making decorations and decorating a Christmas tree. For ideas on construction of symbols, see the illustration below.

Additional Ideas for This Service

If you have additional time and/or resources, you may wish to consider some of the following suggestions for alteration of the basic service:

Hymns. Substitute standard hymns or folk hymns for those suggested in the basic service. *Standard Hymns:* Any of the hymns in the Advent section of your hymnal. *Folk Hymns:* "Advent Carol"; "Advent Proclamation"; "When You Least Expect Him"; "Here We Go A-Caroling" (all in *Avery and Marsh Songbook*); "Wonderful"; "Take Courage" (both in *Gold, Incense and Myrrh*); "Locusts and Wild Honey" (*Locusts and Wild Honey*).

Advent Wreath. Light the first, second, third, and fourth candles during the service.

Solo. Have a soloist sing "New World Coming" (*Exodus Songbook*).

Movie. You may wish to use the movie *The Mark of the Clown* (16mm, color, 15 minutes, produced by Faith and Fantasy, Inc.), which shows a joyously celebrative worship service utilizing many symbols of the Christian faith. For information on film rentals, see "Movies" in Part Three of this book.

ORDER OF WORSHIP

Call to Worship *(responsively)*
 It is a season of expectation!
 It is the time when the Light of the World is on the horizon!
 Let us worship God together, so that the Light may shine in our lives.

Hymn: "Break Forth, O Living Light of God"

Prayer of Reflection *(unison)*

 O God, the world is changing. The Light of your Son is going to shine upon the darkness of the world. This Light can brighten up the dark corners of our lives.

 Open our eyes, so that we may see the Light. Guide our feet, so that we may walk in the sunshine of your love. Prepare our hearts and minds for the coming of your Son our Lord, in whose name we pray. Amen.

Offering and Doxology

Scripture: Isaiah 62:10-12; Deuteronomy 6:4-9

Probe of the Word: Symbols of Jesus' Life
 Divide the group into teams of two or three persons. Give each team materials for making Christmas decorations. Make the decorations shown in the illustration and others that you may wish to add in order to represent other aspects of Jesus' life. After all the teams have finished this activity, have everyone assemble to decorate the Christmas tree. Have participants hang the ornaments in the order given below. As each category of ornaments is hung, comment on its significance as indicated in the following explanation:
 (1) **STAR**—symbol of Jesus' birth; indicates universal importance of the Nativity; (2) **CANDLE**—symbol of the way in which the Light of the World (Jesus) can lead people out of the darkness of sin; (3) **DOVE**—symbol of God's Spirit descending upon Jesus at his baptism; (4) **FISH**—symbol for Jesus Christ and the Christian community; derived from the Greek word "ICHTHUS" ("fish"), which is an acronym for the Greek words for "Jesus Christ, God's Son, our Savior"; (5) **BREAD** and **CUP**—symbols for Holy Communion and for the Christian community; (6) **SUN**—symbol for the Resurrection.
 If you use additional symbols, add your own explanations for the symbols you choose to add.
 After you have finished decorating the tree, have the group pray: *O God, thank you for the great gift of Jesus Christ, whose life we have symbolized in our decorations. As we prepare to celebrate his birth, open us up to the light that he can give to our lives. Amen.*

Hymn: "The People That in Darkness Sat"

Benediction *(to be said by the worship leader)*
 Go forth to walk in the sunshine of the Spirit! Get ready for the festival of Christmas! Amen.

WORSHIP SERVICE NO. 16: "THE FESTIVAL OF CHRISTMAS"
(Christmas Sunday or Christmas Week)

Guidelines for the Basic Service

Purpose: To give persons an opportunity to worship God as they celebrate the birth of Jesus.

Resources and Materials Needed: Bibles; hymnals; a birthday cake; juice; cookies; balloons and other party items (optional)

Hymns. The two suggested hymns are found in many hymnals. Alternative ideas are given in "Additional Ideas for This Service."

The Gloria Patri. This part of the service is a response to the prayer of celebration. For information on alternative forms of the Gloria Patri, see "Additional Hymns and Service Music" in Part Three of this book.

Offering and Doxology. This section is optional, but it is recommended that it be included (see "Probe of the Word" in the basic service). For ideas on Doxologies, see "Additional Hymns and Service Music" in Part Three of this book.

Scripture. Isaiah 9:2, 6-7 is a prophecy of the coming of the Messiah. Luke 2:1-20 is part of Luke's narrative of the Nativity story. The TEV is preferred for both selections.

Probe of the Word. This part of the service is a birthday party for Jesus. Prior to the service, secure a birthday cake and refreshments. You may wish to go "all out" by having the words "Happy Birthday, Jesus" on the cake and adding candles (perhaps twenty candles—one for each century since Jesus' birth). Other ideas: balloons, posters, and other room decorations; party horns and noisemakers.

Additional Ideas for This Service

If you have additional time and/or resources, you may wish to consider some of the following suggestions for alteration of the basic service.

Hymns. Substitute standard hymns or folk hymns for those suggested in the basic service. *Standard Hymns:* Any of the hymns in the Christmas section of your hymnal. *Folk Hymns:* "Christmas Peace" (*The Genesis Songbook*); "Born Again"; "Give a Little Something Special"; "Mary, Mary" (all in *Avery and Marsh Songbook*); "A Child Is Born" (*Locusts and Wild Honey*); "Song of Glory"; "Wonderful"; "Sing of Birth"; "Take Courage"; "No Longer Alone"; "He Comes" (all in *Gold, Incense and Myrrh*).

Advent Wreath. Light the first four candles and then the Christ candle during the service.

Solo. Have a soloist sing "O What a Happening" (*Gold, Incense and Myrrh*).

Movies. You may wish to use one of the following movies: (1) *Christ Is Born* (16mm, color, 54 minutes, produced by ABC). A film that uses scenes from the Holy Land and narrative by actor John Huston to tell the Biblical story from the time of Abraham to the birth of Jesus. (2) *Christmas Bus* (16mm, color, 20 minutes, produced by Family Films). A film that shows how people on a city bus discover the true meaning of Christmas when they reach out and relate to one another. (3) *An Old Box* (16mm, color, 8 minutes, produced by the National Film Board of Canada). A film fantasy about an old crone who discovers the meaning of Christmas by fashioning a music box from a discarded box found in the trash. (4) *The World of Jesus Christ* (16mm, color, 42 minutes, produced by ABC). A film that utilizes various musical selections and 120 art works to tell the story of Christ.

For information on film rentals, see "Movies" in Part Three of this book.

ORDER OF WORSHIP

Call to Worship *(responsively)*
It is time to celebrate the birth of Jesus the Christ!
We are filled with joy and excitement!
Let us worship God together as we enjoy this festival of Christmas.

Hymn: "O Come, All Ye Faithful"

Prayer of Celebration *(unison)*

O God, we thank you for the gift of Jesus the Christ. We praise you for sending your Son to enlighten our lives and show us the way that leads to happiness and hope.

We celebrate this special season with songs of joy and prayers of praise. We welcome one another with happy hugs and words of love. We feast on fancy foods. We shower one another with gifts.

Be present with us in our singing and our celebrating, so that we may share the true spirit of Christmas with one and all, through Jesus our Lord who comes to us on Christmas Day and every day. Amen.

The Gloria Patri

Scripture: Isaiah 9:2, 6-7; Luke 2:1-20

Probe of the Word: A Birthday Party for Jesus

Have everyone gather around the birthday cake. Light the candles, and then have everyone pause to make a silent "Christmas wish"—a prayer for peace in the world, a prayer for someone who is ill, or some other prayer for a special blessing for someone in need. Then blow out the candles. Next have everyone sing "Happy Birthday" to Jesus. Then cut the cake, and serve the cake, juice, and cookies.

After everyone has finished the refreshments, have an affirmation of the birth of Jesus. Say in a loud voice: *Hallelujah! Jesus Christ is born!* and have everyone respond with applause and/or noisemakers.

In preparation for the offering, have a discussion of how the group can make the season happier for some family or individual by giving food and/or a gift. Have participants contribute money or pledges of money for this purpose.

Offering and Doxology

Prayer of Dedication *(unison)*
O God, we offer these gifts and pledges as our thanksgiving to you for your gift of Jesus the Christ. Inspire our hearts, so that we may share the joy of this season with persons who are in need. Amen.

Hymn: "In the Bleak Midwinter"

Benediction *(to be said by the worship leader)*
Go forth to share the spirit of Christmas! Take the gift of Jesus' love to one and all! Amen.

WORSHIP SERVICE NO. 17: "COME, LORD JESUS!"
(Following Christmas)

Guidelines for the Basic Service

Purpose: To give persons an opportunity to participate in a worship service in which they learn about meditation.

Resources and Materials Needed: Bibles; hymnals; record player and records or cassette player and pre-recorded tapes of music (optional)

Hymns. The two suggested hymns are found in many hymnals. Alternative ideas are given in "Additional Hymns and Service Music" in Part Three of this book.

Offering and Doxology. This section is optional. For ideas on Doxologies, see "Additional Hymns and Service Music" in Part Three of this book.

Scripture. First Kings 19:1-13 tells of Elijah's discovery of the voice of God in a moment of silent meditation. The story provides a model for meditation by showing how Elijah becomes renewed and enabled to face a stressful situation by seeking God in the quietness of a special place. Deuteronomy 30:11-14 tells us that we do not have to search far and wide for God's presence, since we can find God's will for us within the depths of our own being. The TEV is preferred for the first selection and the RSV for the second.

Probe of the Word. This part of the service is designed to give worshipers an opportunity to participate in a meditation experience. It is recommended that you consider using soft background music for this experience. The music should be quiet, peaceful, and non-distracting (don't use familiar "hum-along" selections!). A couple of good possibilities: Samuel Barber's *Adagio for Strings*; Ralph Vaughan-Williams' *Fantasy on a Theme of Thomas Tallis*.

Additional Ideas for This Service

If you have additional time and/or resources, you may wish to consider some of the following suggestions for alteration of the basic service:

Hymns. Substitute standard hymns or folk hymns for those suggested in the basic service. Alternatives for the *first* hymn: (1) *Standard Hymns:* "Come, Thou Almighty King"; "Immortal, Invisible, God Only Wise"; "Come Holy Ghost, Our Hearts Inspire"; "Holy Spirit, Truth Divine." (2) *Folk Hymns:* "We're Here to be Happy"; "Canticle for Pentecost" (both in *The Genesis Songbook*); "Psalm of Thanksgiving" (*Exodus Songbook*).

Alternatives for the *second* hymn: (1) *Standard Hymns:* "Spirit of God, Descend Upon My Heart"; "Master, Speak! Thy Servant Heareth"; "God, Thou Who Touchest Earth With Beauty"; "Sweet Hour of Prayer." (2) *Folk Hymns:* "If There Is a Holy Spirit"; "When I'm Feeling Lonely" (both in *Avery and Marsh Songbook*); "God Gives His People Strength" (*Joy Is Like the Rain*); "The Church Within Us" (*The Genesis Songbook*).

Solo. Have a soloist sing "What Makes the Wind Blow?" (*Avery and Marsh Songbook* and *The Genesis Songbook*) or "Listen" (*Listen*).

Recorded Music. Use John Denver's song "Looking for Space" (from his RCA album *Windsong*) as a prelude, offertory, or postlude.

Movie. You may wish to use the movie *Search, Christian Encounter* (16mm, color, 8 minutes, produced by TeleKETICS), which features short sequences raising questions about subjects such as defining God, finding Christ in everyday events, and talking to God. For information on film rentals, see "Movies" in Part Three of this book.

ORDER OF WORSHIP

Call to Worship (to be said by the worship leader)

Let us worship God together. Let us seek God in this service, so that we may learn how to discover God's spirit in the depths of our souls.

Hymn: "O Come, and Dwell in Me"

Prayer of Reflection (unison)

O God, we know that you walk with us on the pathways of our lives. We pause now as we ask you to wait with us in this moment of meditation.

Speak to us in this space of time. Be the sound in our silence. Invade our lives with your loving spirit and fill us to the brim with your powerful presence.

Open us up to the joys of being joined to you. Dispel the darkness of our lives and free us for true communion with you, through Jesus Christ our Lord. Amen.

Offering and Doxology

Scripture: 1 Kings 19:1-13; Deuteronomy 30:11-14

Probe of the Word: A Meditation Experience

Tell participants that they are about to go on a meditation journey. Have everyone seated in a circle. Ask everyone to get comfortable. Then begin the music. As the music plays, give these—or similar—directions at an unhurried pace, with plenty of pauses: *Think of some activity that relaxes you. . . . Let your mind linger on this activity. . . . Now notice your breathing. . . . Breathe deeply and slowly, in and out, in and out. . . . Relax and listen to the music. . . . Imagine that you are part of the music. . . . Now fill your mind with colors . . . calm and peaceful greens . . . cool, refreshing blues . . . bright, warm yellows. . . . Now picture a small light in the midst of the yellow glow. . . . Let the light become a part of you. . . . Imagine the light shining deep within your soul. . . . Now picture at the center of the light the face of Jesus. . . . Gaze at his face. . . . Meditate on his face. . . . See the love and compassion in his eyes. . . . Now concentrate on the word "Jesus." . . . Say the word over and over in your mind. . . . If your mind wanders, gently bring it back. . . . Now relax completely. . . . Let the love of Jesus flood in upon your mind. . . . Look within your mind and feel his presence. . . . Now ask Jesus to bless your life. . . . Ask him to give you strength . . . and joy . . . and peace. . . . Now sit silently for a few moments. . . . Let the music swell up in your consciousness. . . . Slowly, . . . slowly . . . open your eyes . . . Now stretch your arms and legs. . . . Now relax your whole body. . . . Sit for a few moments with your eyes open. . . . Now reach out and join hands with persons next to you. Let us all say together: "Come, Lord Jesus. . . . Come into my life. . . . Amen."*

Hymn: "Breathe on Me, Breath of God"

Benediction (to be said by the worship leader)

Go forth with the spirit of Christ in your hearts! Center down on the indwelling spirit, so that God may speak to you wherever you are! Amen.

WORSHIP SERVICE NO. 18: "SHARING THE FAITH"
(Following Christmas)

Guidelines for the Basic Service

Purpose: To give persons an opportunity to participate in a worship service in which they learn how to share their Christian faith.

Resources and Materials Needed: Bibles; hymnals; pencils and paper; cassette recorder, microphone, and tape (optional); record player and records of "mood music" (optional)

Hymns. The two suggested hymns are found in many hymnals. Alternative ideas are given in "Additional Ideas for This Service."

Offering and Doxology. This section is optional. For ideas on Doxologies, see "Additional Hymns and Service Music" in Part Three of this book.

Scripture. Isaiah 42:1-9 is a prediction of the coming Messiah. The emphasis in this selection is on the gifts that the Messiah will bring to the world—justice, enlightenment, healing, and liberation. John 1:14-19, sometimes referred to as the Prologue to John's Gospel, points to the Incarnation as the source of light and new life for humanity. The TEV is recommended for both selections.

Probe of the Word. This part of the service is designed to give participants an opportunity to develop creative ways of sharing their faith by producing "commercials" for Jesus. In preparation for this activity, you should write out the words to five or six TV and/or radio commercials for well-known products.

Additional Ideas for This Service

If you have additional time and/or resources, you may wish to consider some of the following suggestions for alteration of the basic service:

Hymns. Substitute standard hymns or folk hymns for the hymns suggested in the basic service. *Standard Hymns:* Any of the hymns in the Christmas or Epiphany sections of your hymnal. *Folk Hymns:* "Christmas Peace"; "You Can Tell the World" (*The Genesis Songbook*); "Born Again"; "Give a Little Something Special"; "Mary, Mary"; "Starlight"; "Let's God" (all in *Avery and Marsh Songbook*); "A Child Is Born" (*Locusts and Wild Honey*); "Song of Glory"; "Wonderful"; "Sing of Birth"; "Take Courage"; "No Longer Alone"; "He Comes" (all in *Gold, Incense and Myrrh*); "You Are the Salt of the Earth" (*Exodus Songbook*).

Solo. Have a soloist sing the song "Vincent" from Don McLean's United Artists album *American Pie*. Make the following changes in order to make the song into a "commercial" for Jesus: change "Vincent" to "Jesus" and change the phrase "took your life" to "gave your life." Another good solo: "Shine, Star!" (*Avery and Marsh Songbook*).

Movies. You may wish to use one of the following movies: (1) *Parable* (16mm, color, 22 minutes, produced by Rolf Forsberg). A film about how a clown (a Christ figure) liberates those who follow him. (2) *Oh Happy Day* (16mm, color, 10 minutes, produced by Hakan Ohlsson Forlag). A film about a street sweeper who has a Christ-like effect on four people who are liberated by their encounters with him. (3) *Everyone, Everywhere* (16mm, color, 15 minutes, produced by TeleKETICS). A film in which Mother Teresa challenges people to respond to needy people. (4) *The Antkeeper* (16mm, color, 30 minutes, produced by Rolf Forsberg). An allegorical film about a gardener whose son becomes an ant and gives the other ants wings.

For information on film rentals, see "Movies" in Part Three of this book.

ORDER OF WORSHIP

Call to Worship *(responsively)*
It is the season of joy!
It is time to tell the world about Christ!
Let us worship God together. Let us proclaim the good news. Let us tell all people about the liberating love of Christ.

Hymn: "Joy to the World"

Prayer of Celebration *(unison)*
O God, with joy and hope we celebrate this happy season. We thank you for sending Jesus the Christ to live among us. We want to tell everyone about the new way of life that we have found in him.
Inspire our minds, so that we will know what to say. Strengthen us, so that we will be able to speak boldly and clearly. Send your spirit to invade our lives, so that our actions will match our words.
Help us to witness with joy and power—in the name of the One who came as the true witness to your word. Amen.

Offering and Doxology

Scripture: Isaiah 42:1-9; John 1:1-14

Probe of the Word: Writing Commercials for Jesus Christ
Point out that the Gospels could be viewed as "commercials for Christ." Emphasize the intention of the Gospel writers by reading Luke 1:1-4 and John 23:25. Then have the participants brainstorm for a few minutes on the qualities of Jesus that they would like to share with other people. Next read some TV and/or radio commercials as examples of the ways in which modern advertising communicators try to convince people that they should be interested in certain products.
Divide the group into teams of two or three persons. Have the teams work on creating "commercials" to communicate the qualities of Jesus that were mentioned in the discussion. Tell team members that they may adapt commercials that they have heard or write entirely new material. If you have recording equipment available, have teams record their creations. An extra touch could be added by playing music softly in the background while scripts are being recorded.
After all the teams have finished this activity, have a period of sharing. Discuss how skills acquired in this activity might help individual participants as they attempt to share their faith with other persons.

Hymn: "Go, Tell It on the Mountain"

Benediction *(responsively)*
You are Christ's people! The spirit of God has changed your lives!
We want to share that life-changing spirit with everyone!
Then go out from this place to tell the world that the Savior has come and that life can be filled with happiness and joy—through Jesus Christ our Lord! Amen.

WORSHIP SERVICE NO. 19: "DEALING WITH RACISM"

Guidelines for the Basic Service

Purpose: To give persons an opportunity to participate in a worship service in which they learn how to deal with racist feelings and actions.

Resources and Materials Needed: Bibles; hymnals; pencils and paper; refreshments

Hymns. The two suggested hymns are found in many hymnals. Alternative ideas are given in "Additional Ideas for This Service."

Scripture. Micah 6:6-8 points out that our worship of God is meaningless if we fail to do what God requires: to act in a spirit of justice, to show constant love, and to live in a right relationship with God. First John 4:7-12 epitomizes the main message of this epistle—we should love one another as God loves us. The TEV is preferred for both selections.

Probe of the Word. This part of the service is designed to sensitize participants to the harmful effects of prejudice and to help them become aware of ways in which prejudice may be overcome. The main activity is a simulation game that shows participants how it feels to be discriminated against.

Additional Ideas for This Service

If you have additional time and/or resources, you may wish to consider some of the following suggestions for alteration of the basic service:

Hymns. Substitute standard hymns or folk hymns for those suggested in the basic service. Alternatives for the *first* hymn: (1) *Standard Hymn:* "In Christ There Is No East or West." (2) *Folk Hymns:* "They'll Know We Are Christians by Our Love" (*Songbook for Saints and Sinners, The Genesis Songbook*, and other collections).

Alternatives for the *second* hymn: *Folk Hymns:* "Tear Down the Walls" (in "Additional Hymns and Service Music" in Part Three of this book); "Evertying is Beautiful"; "Wonderful World, Beautiful People"; "Love One Another"; "There's a Quiet Understanding"; "What the World Needs Now Is Love"; "Break Not the Circle" (all in *Exodus Songbook*); "I'd Like to Teach the World to Sing"; "We Shall Overcome"; "What a Great Thing It Is"; "If I Had a Hammer" (all in *The Genesis Songbook*).

Solo. Have a soloist sing "Who's That Guy" (*Avery and Marsh Songbook*).

Recorded Music. Use one of the following songs as a prelude, offertory, and/or postlude: "Love (1 Corinthians 13)" from Joni Mitchell's Geffen Records album *Wild Things Run Fast*; or "Ebony and Ivory" from Paul McCartney's Columbia album *Tug of War*. For a slide-and-tape presentation, use either of these songs with slides of people of various races, ethnic groups, nationalities, ages, and so forth.

Movies. You may wish to use one of the following movies: (1) *A Friendly Game* (16mm, black & white, 10 minutes, produced by Robert Glatzer). A symbolic film about a black man and a white man playing a game of chess. (2) *Bill Cosby on Prejudice* (16mm, color, 24 minutes, produced by Pyramid Films). A satirical monologue that presents a scathing parody of bigotry. (3) *Let the Rain Settle It* (16mm, color, 13 minutes, produced by Franciscan Communications Center). A film about a white boy and a black boy who begin a friendship during a twenty-four-hour period when they are thrown together.

For information on film rentals, see "Movies" in Part Three of this book.

ORDER OF WORSHIP

Call to Worship *(responsively)*

God loves us! And God calls us to love one another!

But we are separated by differences that divide us. We are kept apart by distrust and prejudice. It is difficult for us to love all people.

God will strengthen us, so that we can overcome the gulfs that separate us. Let us worship God, who can unite us in love.

Hymn: "Love Divine, All Loves Excelling"

Prayer of Confession *(unison)*

O God, we know that you want all people to live together in love and harmony. We are aware that you want us to look beyond our differences and become brothers and sisters in the family of humanity.

We confess that we have failed to follow your way. We have distrusted one another. We have accented our differences. We have built walls of fear and distrust.

Forgive our sins of separation. Free us from our prisons of prejudice. Open us up, so that we may accept all people as our brothers and sisters. Amen.

Words of Forgiveness and Hope *(to be said by the worship leader)*

You are forgiven and accepted. From now on, love and care for everybody, just as God loves and cares for you.

Offering and Doxology

Scripture: Micah 6:6-8; 1 John 4:7-12

Probe of the Word: Dealing With Prejudice

Divide the participants into two groups on the basis of some particular physical characteristic (examples: (1) people with brown eyes; people whose eyes are another color; (2) people with blonde hair; people whose hair is another color; (3) people with light skin; people with dark skin). Designate one group as "superior" and the other group as "inferior." Inform everyone that the "superior" group is to receive preferential treatment. Serve the first half of the refreshments. Give the "superior" group generous servings and the "inferior" group meager servings. Then have an informal period of conversation. During this period, the "superior" persons are to discriminate against the "inferior" persons by ignoring them, by laughing at them, and so forth. Then reverse the roles, serve the second half of the refreshments, and repeat the conversation period.

Afterward, have participants discuss how it felt to be discriminated against. Continue the discussion by relating the activity to prejudiced behavior in everyday life. Conclude by having participants brainstorm some ways in which they can work to eliminate prejudice in their own lives and in society in general.

Hymn: "These Things Shall Be"

Benediction *(to be said by the worship leader)*

Go forth to love and care for all people! Amen.

WORSHIP SERVICE NO. 20: "HOPE OF THE WORLD"

Guidelines for the Basic Service

Purpose: To help persons experience the Christian hope in a worship service.

Resources and Materials Needed: Bibles; hymnals; collage materials; newspaper headlines, poster board, glue, scissors; room decorations: flowers, balloons, posters, and so forth; pencils, paper, and envelopes; offering plate(s) (optional)

Hymns. The two suggested hymns are found in many hymnals. Alternative ideas are given in "Additional Ideas for This Service."

Offering and Doxology. This section is optional, but it is recommended that it be included. For ideas on Doxologies, see "Additional Hymns and Service Music" in Part Three of this book.

Scripture. Romans 5:1-5 is one of Paul's affirmations of the hope that a Christian has even in the midst of troubles. Romans 8:18-25 is a similar affirmation, with an added discussion of the suffering and decadence found throughout all creation. The TEV is recommended for both selections.

Probe of the Word. This part of the service is designed to be an acted-out illustration of the two Biblical passages. The probe has two parts: (1) a discussion of things that make participants sad and discouraged; and (2) an activity in which gifts of hope are offered. In preparation for this probe, make a collage out of newspaper headlines that tell of bad news. Display the collage in a conspicuous place and surround it with festive decorations—flowers, balloons, inspirational posters, and so forth.

Additional Ideas for This Service

If you have additional time and/or resources, you may wish to consider some of the following suggestions for alteration of the basic service:

Hymns. Substitute standard hymns or folk hymns for those suggested in the basic service. Alternatives for the *first* hymn: (1) *Standard Hymns:* "God of Our Life"; "God of the Ages, by Whose Hand." *Folk Hymns:* "Transformation"; "Morning Has Broken"; "We're Here to Be Happy" (all in *The Genesis Songbook*).

Alternatives for the *second* hymn: (1) *Standard Hymns:* "Give to the Winds Thy Fears"; "Have Faith in God, My Heart." (2) *Folk Hymns:* "The Morning After"; "You Are the Salt of the Earth"; "New World Coming" (all in *Exodus Songbook*); "Genesis One" (*The Genesis Songbook*); "Moments to Live By" (*Listen*); "Happiness" (*Wherever You Go*); "God Gives His People Strength" (*Joy Is Like the Rain*).

Recorded Music. Use recorded music for a prelude, offertory, and/or postlude. Suggestions: "Diamonds and Pearls" from Kansas' Kirshner Records album *Vinyl Confessions*; "Dweller on the Threshold" from Van Morrison's Warner album *Beautiful Vision*; "Light at the End of the Darkness" from Larry Gatlin's Monument Records album *The Pilgrim*; "Changes IV" from Cat Stevens' A&M album *Teaser and the Firecat*; "Weave Me the Sunshine" from Noel Paul Stookey's Warner album *One Night Stand*; "Sunshine on My Shoulders" from the RCA album *John Denver's Greatest Hits*.

Movies. You may wish to use one of the following movies: (1) *The Cave* (16mm, color, 9 minutes, produced by Counterpoint Films). A film that retells Plato's allegory about a cave (the world) in which some chained prisoners ridicule a returning former prisoner who tells them of the world outside. (2) *Church in the World* (16mm, color, 20 minutes, produced by P.K.). A film that applies the gospel to the needs of the world.

For information on film rentals, see "Movies" in Part Three of this book.

ORDER OF WORSHIP

Call to Worship *(responsively)*
You are God's people! God offers you hope for the future!
We know! Our God is the God of hope, who gives us the promise of a better tomorrow!
Then let us worship God together as we face the future with joy and faith.

Hymn: "Hope of the World"

Prayer of Reflection *(unison)*

O God, you fill our heads and our hearts with exciting visions. You call to us to look beyond the limits that we have set for ourselves. You widen our narrow viewpoints and you push us to be daring dreamers.

We thank you for the hope that you have instilled in our hearts. We praise you for the promises with which you brighten our lives.

Bless us now with the gift of hope, so that we may live our lives in true faith and face the future with confidence, through Jesus Christ our Lord. Amen.

Scripture: Romans 5:1-5; 8:18-25

Probe of the Word: The Gift of Hope

Have everyone focus on the collage. Discuss events and situations referred to in the headlines. Then divide into teams of two or three persons. Have the teams discuss reasons that participants have for feeling distressed or discouraged about themselves and/or their families and friends. Afterward, have everyone assemble together and have voluntary sharing of the team discussions—with the understanding that names do not have to be used in the sharing.

After all have shared, have everyone pray this prayer: *O God, we present to you our own problems and the problems of the world. Strengthen us and give us hope, so that we may trust in you for the future and work to make things better in our lives and in the world. Amen.*

Then give each person a pencil, a piece of paper, and an envelope. Have everyone write for each of the following categories his or her "gift of hope"—a wish for something good in the future. Tell the group that the inclusion of their names and or names of other persons is optional and that the envelopes will be opened and read in the group's Easter Sunday worship service.

1. My Hope for Myself
2. My Hope for a Member of My Family or a Friend
3. My Hope for the World

Have participants seal the envelopes and place them—along with any offerings of money—in the offering plate(s) or on the altar during the offering. Keep the envelopes for use on Easter Sunday.

Offering and Doxology

Hymn: "Amazing Grace! How Sweet the Sound"

Benediction *(to be said by the worship leader)*
Go forth in hope! Do all you can to make your dreams come true! Amen.

WORSHIP SERVICE NO. 21: "A NEW LIFE-STYLE"

Guidelines for the Basic Service

Purpose: To give persons an opportunity to participate in a worship service in which they become more aware of what it means to have a Christian life-style.

Resources and Materials Needed: Bibles; hymnals; pencils and paper; newsprint and markers, *or* chalkboard, chalk, and an eraser

Hymns. The two suggested hymns are found in many hymnals. Alternative ideas are given in "Additional Ideas for This Service."

Offering and Doxology. This section is optional. For ideas on Doxologies, see "Additional Hymns and Service Music" in Part Three of this book.

Scripture. Deuteronomy 30:15-20 contains Moses' admonition to the people of Israel to "choose life" by following God's commandments. Second Corinthians 5:16-17 is a reminder that the Christian is a new person with new perspectives. Exodus 20:1-17 and Matthew 5:1-12 present two sets of guidelines for God's people (the Ten Commandments and the Beatitudes). The TEV is preferred for all the selections.

Probe of the Word. This part of the service is a simulation game, in which participants draw up the "blueprint" for a new society. You should give special attention to the subsequent discussion, so that participants will be able to make a meaningful transition from the simulation game to a consideration of their own individual life-styles.

Additional Ideas for This Service

If you have additional time and/or resources, you may wish to consider some of the following suggestions for alteration of the basic service:

Hymns. Substitute standard hymns or folk hymns for those suggested in the basic service. Alternatives for the *first* hymn: (1) *Standard Hymn:* "God of the Ages, by Whose Hand"; (2) *Folk Hymns:* "Morning Has Broken" (*The Genesis Songbook*); "Jesus Is Life"; "In Him We Live" (both in *Abba, Father*).

Alternatives for the *second* hymn: (1) *Standard Hymns:* "If Thou But Suffer God to Guide Thee"; "Through All the Changing Scenes of Life"; (2) *Folk Hymns:* "Day by Day"; "Genesis One"; "Transformation"; "The Church Within Us" (all in *The Genesis Songbook*); "Somewhere"; "On Our Way"; "You Are the Salt of the Earth"; "New World Coming" (all in *Exodus Songbook*); "Come as a Child"; "Every Morning Is Easter Morning" (both in *Avery and Marsh Songbook*); "Happiness"; "Anything Happens" (both in *Wherever You Go*); "Moments to Live By"; "New Life, New Creation" (both in *Listen*).

Movies. Use one of the following movies: (1) *Bonhoeffer: A Life of Challenge* (16mm, color, 28 minutes, produced by the Bonhoeffer Project—Panagraph). A film about the famous German pastor who lost his life because of his opposition to Hitler. (2) *How Good Life Can Be* (16mm, color, 24 minutes, produced by the Lutheran Brotherhood). A film about self-realization through giving of oneself.

For information on film rentals, see "Movies" in Part Three of this book.

Recorded Music. Use recorded music for a prelude, offertory, and/or postlude. Suggestions: "There's a World" by Neil Young on his Reprise album *Harvest*; "Amazing Grace" by Joan Baez on her A&M album *From Every Stage*; "Sweet Surrender" by John Denver on his RCA album *Back Home Again* or by Peter, Paul and Mary on their Warner Brothers album *Reunion*.

ORDER OF WORSHIP

Call to Worship *(responsively)*
    You are God's people! God has created you, and God offers you new life!
    We want to live our lives as God's people! We want to find a new way of living!
    Then let us worship God together, so that we may become new creations through Christ our Lord.

Hymn: "God of Our Life"

Prayer of Reflection *(unison)*

    O God, we are aware that you offer us new life and new possibilities. We want to say "yes" to you. We want to be open to the new world that is within our grasp.

    Yet we are hampered by the hold that the past has on us. We fasten on to the familiar. We are overcome by old ways and habits. We allow ourselves to be closed in by those things that make us comfortable.

    Forgive us for our foolish faith in the past. Save us from our attempts to find security in what seems safe and comfortable. Show us the way that leads to new life, and give us the courage to set out on the journey. Amen.

Offering and Doxology

Scripture: Deuteronomy 30:15-20; 2 Corinthians 5:16-17

Probe of the Word: Creating a New Life-Style
    Tell participants that they are going to be involved in a simulation game in which they will create a new society. The situation is as follows: They have been shipwrecked on an island. Their only printed resource is a copy of the Bible. Their task is to draw up plans for their society. Their goal is to create the best society possible.
    Tell the participants that they may use any part of the Bible as their guide; suggest that they may want to give particular attention to the Ten Commandments (Exodus 20:1-17) and the Beatitudes (Matthew 5:1-12). Then divide the group into teams of two or three persons and have them brainstorm ideas. The following questions may be used as discussion starters:

    1. How will the economic system be set up? How will it be supervised?
    2. What rules and laws will the society have? How will these be enforced?
    3. What behavior will be acceptable? What behavior will be unacceptable? Why?
    4. How will leaders be chosen? What powers will they have?
    5. What kind of religion will the society have? Describe it in detail.
    6. What ideas do you have regarding the following: war and peace; theft; murder; cheating; greed; honesty; ecology and natural resources; use of money; use of time; relationships among people; marriage and divorce; children; wealth and poverty; needy persons; sick people; elderly people?

    Afterward, collate and discuss responses. Then discuss how things learned in this activity might help individual persons make changes in their life-styles.

Hymn: "These Things Shall Be"

Benediction *(to be said by the worship leader)*
    Go forth in God's grace and seek out the ideal Christian life-style! Amen.

WORSHIP SERVICE NO. 22: "INTO THE LIGHT"

Guidelines for the Basic Service

Purpose: To give persons an opportunity to participate in a worship service in which they gain a better understanding of the Biblical concepts of light and darkness.

Resources and Materials Needed: Bibles; hymnals; pencils and paper; a room that can be darkened *or* blindfolds; newsprint and markers, *or* chalkboard, chalk, and eraser; record player or cassette player (optional); candles and matches (optional)

Hymns. The two suggested hymns are found in many hymnals. Alternative ideas are given in "Additional Ideas for This Service."

Offering and Doxology. This section is optional. For ideas on Doxologies, see "Additional Hymns and Service Music" in Part Three of this book.

Scripture. John 1:1-9; 3:19-21; 8:12; 12:35-36, 46. These selections from the Gospel of John present one of John's main themes—the contrast between the light of Jesus' way and the darkness of a sinful world. The TEV is preferred.

Probe of the Word. This part of the service is designed to give participants a deeper understanding of the Biblical concepts of light and darkness. It includes an activity in which participants give examples of events, actions, and situations that illustrate darkness and those that illustrate light. It also includes a "rite of passage" by which participants actually go from a state of darkness to a state of light.

Additional Ideas for This Service

If you have additional time and/or resources, you may wish to consider some of the following suggestions for alteration of the basic service:

Hymns. Substitute standard hymns or folk hymns for those suggested in the basic service. Alternatives for the *first* hymn: (1) *Standard Hymns:* "Spirit of Life, in This New Dawn"; "Light of the World, We Hail Thee"—change "men" to "all"; (2) *Folk Hymns:* "Morning Has Broken" (*The Genesis Songbook*); "The Goodness of God Cries Out" *(Locusts and Wild Honey)*; "A Light Has Shone" *(Wherever You Go)*.

Alternatives for the *second* hymn: (1) *Standard Hymn:* "I Heard the Voice of Jesus Say"; (2) *Folk Hymns:* "The Morning After"; "You Are the Salt of the Earth" (both in *Exodus Songbook*); "Starlight"; "Shine, Star!" (both in *Avery and Marsh Songbook*).

Recorded Music: Use recorded music for a postlude, offertory, and/or prelude. Suggestions: "Light of the World" from the Bell Records album of *Godspell*; "Weave Me the Sunshine" by Noel Paul Stookey on his Warner Brothers album *One Night Stand*; "Light at the End of the Darkness" by Larry Gatlin on his Monument Records album *The Pilgrim*; "Here Comes the Sun" by the Beatles on their Apple Records album *The Beatles: 1967-1970*. As an alternative usage, play one of these selections as the group moves from darkness to light during the Probe of the Word.

Solo. Have a soloist sing "You are the Sunshine of My Life" *(Exodus Songbook)*.

Movies. Use one of the following movies: (1) *Light Shines in the Darkness* (16mm, color, 22 minutes, produced by Cathedral Films). A film that uses contemporary art to tell the biblical story from the Crucifixion to the day of Pentecost. (2) *The Cave* (16mm, color, 9 minutes, produced by Counterpoint Films). A film that retells Plato's story of a cave in which chained prisoners ridicule a returning former prisoner who brings them a message about the world that exists outside the cave.

For information on film rentals, see "Movies" in Part Three of this book.

ORDER OF WORSHIP

Call to Worship (*responsively*)
Jesus Christ is the Light of the world!
We have caught a glimpse of that Light! We want it to shine in our lives!
Then let us worship God as we look for that life-giving Light.

Hymn: "Christ, Whose Glory Fills the Skies"

Prayer of Reflection (*unison*)

O God, we know that you are the source of light and life. We thank you for sending your Son to lead us out of darkness. We praise you for the rays of hope that brighten the valleys of our lives.

We admit that we have often preferred darkness to light. We have been content to take cover in the shadows. We have sought satisfaction along unlighted pathways.

Lead us, O God, so that we may discover your light. Shine on the shadows of our lives, so that we may discover your will. Drive out the darkness that clouds our minds, so that we may focus on the One who is the sunshine of our lives. Amen.

Offering and Doxology

Scripture: John 1:1-9; 3:19-21; 8:12; 12:35-37, 46

Probe of the Word: Moving Into the Light

Give everyone a pencil and a piece of paper. Have each person divide his or her sheet into two columns and write "Darkness" at the top of one column and "Light" at the top of the other. Then have persons work individually to write down under the heading "Darkness" some events, actions, and situations that are examples of sinfulness in the world and in their own personal lives and to write down under the heading "Light" some events, actions, and situations that are examples of people (including themselves) who are doing God's will by working to make the world a better place.

After all have finished, collate responses on newsprint or a chalkboard. Then have each person choose from each category one example that he or she will keep in mind to use in the light-to-darkness ritual.

Next darken the room as much as possible or blindfold everyone. Then have individuals take turns at shouting out their examples of "Darkness." Then move from darkness into light by gradually lighting the room with candles or having persons remove their blindfolds one by one. As an added touch, you may wish to play one of the suggested musical selections during this "rite of passage." When the room is completely lighted (or when all blindfolds have been removed), have individuals take turns at shouting out their examples of "Light."

Afterward, use the examples of "Light" and other suggestions that participants wish to make as the basis for a discussion of how group members can fulfill their role as "People of the Light" by taking specific actions to make the world a better place.

Hymn: "Walk in the Light"

Benediction (*to be said by the worship leader*)
Go forth to be God's people! Take God's light to a dark and sinful world! Amen.

WORSHIP SERVICE NO. 23: "GOOD NEWS TO THE POOR"

Guidelines for the Basic Service

Purpose: To help persons discover in worship both their responsibility toward the poor and ways to fulfill that responsibility.

Resources and Materials Needed: Bibles; hymnals; a pencil and a piece of paper for each participant; newsprint and markers, *or* chalkboard, chalk, and eraser

Hymns. The first hymn is found in many hymnals. The folk hymn "The Spirit of the Lord" is in "Additional Hymns and Service Music" in Part Three of this book. Alternative ideas are given in "Additional Ideas for This Service."

Offering and Doxology. This section is optional, but it is preferable that it be included—since it is related to the theme of the service. For ideas on Doxologies, see "Additional Hymns and Service Music" in Part Three of this book.

Scripture. The first line of the Call to Worship is a paraphrase of Proverbs 14:31. The second line refers to Matthew 25:31-40 (used later in the service). This passage is part of Jesus' famous Parable of the Last Judgment which emphasizes the Christian's responsibility toward the needy. Luke 4:14-19 tells of the incident of Jesus' reading of an Isaiah selection in the synagogue. This selection provides a keynote for Jesus' ministry—and for ours!

Probe of the Word. The leader should provide adequate guidance during this activity. Try to help the group and individuals choose actions that are specific, meaningful, and realistic.

Additional Ideas for This Service

If you have additional time and/or resources, you may wish to consider some of the following suggestions for alteration of the basic service:

Hymns. Substitute standard hymns or folk hymns for those suggested in the basic service. *Standard Hymns:* "Lord, Speak to Me"; "O Thou Who Art the Shephard"; "Where Cross the Crowded Ways of Life." *Folk Hymns:* "Choose Life"; "Let the Spirit In" (both in *Genesis Songbook*).

Movies. Before the Probe of the Word, show one of these movies dealing with the Christian's responsibility to help the needy: (1) *Because They Care* (16mm, color, 30 minutes, produced by CBS). A documentary about CROP, the domestic community action program of Church World Service. Shows CROP projects in which persons concerned about world hunger can participate. (2) *Because This Is Where They Live* (16mm, color, 18 minutes, produced by Total Communications Laboratory). The story of Tex Evans' Appalachian Service Project is presented in this documentary about a group of young people who spend their summer vacation repairing the homes of poor families. (3) *Everyone, Everywhere* (16mm, color, 15 minutes, produced by TeleKETICS). A film in which Mother Teresa challenges us to meet Christ by responding to the needs of people who are poor and sick. (4) *Theirs Is the Kingdom* (16mm, color, 5 minutes, produced by Franciscan Communications Center). A fascinating film that deals with the question of motivation for helping the poor.

For information on film rentals, see "Movies" in Part Three of this book.

ORDER OF WORSHIP

Call to Worship (responsively)

My friends, the Old Testament tells us: The person who oppresses the poor insults God, but the person who is kind to the needy honors God.

In the New Testament, Jesus tells us: Whatever we do to the least of our brothers and sisters, we also do to him.

Let us worship God and discover what we can do to help those who are poor and needy.

Hymn: "The Voice of God Is Calling"

Prayer of Confession (unison)

O God, forgive us our failure to understand the great demands of the Gospel. We have not responded sufficiently to the cries of the needy. We have not shared as we should with the poor. We have taken from the bounty of your world without giving enough to those who have so little. Make us discontent with our greediness. Give us the grace to give graciously. Help us always to remember that you love a cheerful giver. Amen.

Words of Forgiveness and Hope (to be said by the worship leader)

My friends, God accepts and forgives us. Our sins of selfishness are no longer held against us. The future is open to us if we will change our ways. As forgiven people, we are called to give to others. Let us answer that call.

Offering and Doxology

Scripture: Luke 4:14-19; Matthew 25:31-40

Probe of the Word: Helping the Poor and Needy

Give each person a pencil and a piece of paper. Have everyone take a few minutes to write down at least one way in which he or she can individually help persons who are poor and needy and at least one way in which the group can help such persons.

Afterward, have each person read his or her responses. Deal with suggestions for individual action first, and then deal with suggestions for group action. Process the responses in the following manner:

(1) Individual Action. Collate the responses. Then say to the group: *Choose from all the suggestions for individual action at least one thing that you will personally pledge to do.* Then pray: *O God, give us the determination and the ability to carry out our individual pledges. Amen.*

(2) Group Action. Collate the responses. Then have the group select from the suggestions for group action at least one thing that they will pledge to do as a group. Make initial plans for this group action. Decide on follow-up plans and action. Then pray: *O God, give us the determination and the ability to carry out our group plans. Amen.*

Hymn: "The Spirit of the Lord"

Benediction (to be said by the worship leader)

Go forth with God's blessing to take aid and hope to a needy world. Amen.

WORSHIP SERVICE NO. 24: "REACHING OUT TO OLDER PERSONS"

Guidelines for the Basic Service

Purpose: To enable persons to discover in worship both an appreciation for older persons and their responsibility to reach out to older persons.

Resources and Materials Needed: Bibles; hymnals; a pencil and two pieces of paper for each person; newsprint and markers, *or* chalkboard, chalk, and eraser

Hymns. The two suggested hymns are found in many hymnals. Alternative ideas are given in "Additional Ideas for This Service."

Offering and Doxology. This section is optional. For ideas on Doxologies, see "Additional Hymns and Service Music" in Part Three of this book.

Scripture. Exodus 20:12 gives one of the Ten Commandments. It calls for respect for parents. The same thought is expressed in the selection from Proverbs 23. The TEV is preferred for both passages.

Probe of the Word. You may find it helpful to give some suggestions of your own for group action. Possibilities include: helping older persons with household chores and yard work; doing grocery shopping for older persons; "adopting" a grandparent; visiting a nursing home; having a party for people in a nursing home.

Additional Ideas for This Service

If you have additional time and/or resources, you may wish to consider some of the following suggestions for alteration of the basic service:

Hymns. Substitute standard hymns or folk hymns for those suggested in the basic service. *Standard Hymns:* "O Master, Let Me Walk With Thee"; "When the Storms of Life Are Raging." *Folk Hymns:* "Come On and Celebrate!" (in "Additional Hymns and Service Music" in Part Three of this book); "Take All the Lost Home" (*A New Commandment*); "Sing Love Songs"; "We Are the Church" (both in *Avery and Marsh Songbook*).

Recorded Music. Choose from the following recordings one for use as a prelude and one for use as a postlude: Joan Baez' version of John Prine's "Hello In There" (from her A&M album *Diamonds and Rust*); Simon and Garfunkel's "Old Friends" (from their Columbia album *Bookends*); John Denver's "Friends With You" (from his RCA album *Aerie*); Neil Diamond's "Morningside" (from his MCA album *Moods*); James Taylor's version of Carole King's "You've Got a Friend" (from his Warner album *Greatest Hits*).

Movies. Before the Probe of the Word, show one of these movies about the concerns of the aged: (1) *Peege* (16mm, color, 28 minutes, produced by Phoenix Films). A film about how a young college student communicates with his grandmother who is in a nursing home. (2) *Portrait of Grandpa Doc* (16mm, color, 28 minutes, produced by Phoenix Films). This companion movie to *Peege* shows the lasting influence that a grandfather has on his grandson. (3) *The Shopping Bag Lady* (16mm, color, 21 minutes, produced by Learning Corporation of America). Story of how a teenager learns to appreciate an old woman who is a street dweller.

For information on film rentals, see "Movies" in Part Three of this book.

ORDER OF WORSHIP

Call to Worship *(to be said by the worship leader)*

As we gather together, let us be aware of the gifts that God gives us through the lives of older persons. Let us praise God who makes it possible for us to learn from those who have acquired the experience and wisdom that come from many years of living.

Hymn: "O Thou Who Art the Shepherd"

Prayer of Reflection *(unison)*

O God, we thank you for the older persons whom we are privileged to know. Show us how to learn the lessons of life and love that they can teach us. Enable us to listen lovingly so that we may be sensitive to the songs in their souls and the melodies in their memories.

When they are lonely, help us to respond in love. When they are fearful, help us to fill their lives with faith. When they are feeling hopeless, help us to be their source of hope and healing. Help us to offer the tender touch, the caring caress, the word of welcome, through Jesus Christ our Lord. Amen.

Offering and Doxology

Scripture: Exodus 20:12; Proverbs 23: 22, 24, 25

Probe of the Word: Reaching Out to Older People

Part One: A Mind-Journey. Give each person a pencil and a piece of paper. Ask everyone to imagine that he or she is seventy years old and to respond to the following questions as if he or she were actually that age: *(1) What kind of house are you living in? (2) How would you describe a typical day in your life? (3) What physical illnesses or ailments do you have? (4) How do you feel about what you have accomplished thus far in your life? (5) Who are your friends? (6) How do teenagers treat you? (7) What do you look forward to in your life? (8) What makes you feel happy? (9) What makes you feel sad? (10) What is your biggest problem?*

Afterward, share responses. Discuss particularly what this activity reveals about how it feels to be an older person.

Part Two: An Action Plan. Give each person another piece of paper. Have everyone take a few minutes to write down one way in which he or she can be helpful to—or relate better with—an older person and one way in which the group can be helpful to older persons.

Afterward, have each person share his or her responses. Collate the responses. Deal with the two categories separately. Have each person choose from the suggestions for *individual* action at least one thing that he or she will pledge to do. Then have the group decide on at least one thing that they will do *as a group.* Conclude by making specific plans for group action.

Hymn: "Lord, Whose Love Through Humble Service"

Benediction *(to be said by the worship leader)*

Go forth in love. Aid the aged. Care for the lonely. Share yourself. Amen.

WORSHIP SERVICE NO. 25: "A GOOD INFLUENCE"

Guidelines for the Basic Service

Purpose: To give persons an opportunity to participate in a worship service in which they become more aware of the influence that they can have on people.

Resources and Materials Needed: Bibles; hymnals

Hymns. The two suggested hymns are found in many hymnals. Alternative ideas are given in "Additional Ideas for This Service."

Offering and Doxology. This section is optional. For ideas on Doxologies, see "Additional Hymns and Service Music" in Part Three of this book.

Scripture. In Matthew 18:6-7, Jesus cautions people against setting a bad example and leading other people astray. In 1 Corinthians 8:9-13, Paul warns people about the bad influence that they can have when they are involved in behavior that is not wrong in and of itself but may nevertheless have a bad influence on someone who might misinterpret the behavior. Matthew 5:19 is an example of Jesus' teaching on the effects of good behavior and bad behavior. The TEV is preferred for all the selections.

Probe of the Word. This part of the service is designed to give participants some insights about how persons can influence one another in positive ways and negative ways. The main activity is a "mini-skit," an open-ended playlet in which the five participants are to role play the unfinished part of the skit. In preparation for this activity, you should choose five persons who are creative and dramatically-inclined and spend some time prior to the service coaching them and discussing the direction in which they want the role play to proceed.

Additional Ideas for This Service

If you have additional time and/or resources you may wish to consider some of the following suggestions for alteration of the basic service:

Hymns. Substitute standard hymns or folk hymns for those suggested in the basic service. Alternatives for the *first* hymn: (1) *Standard Hymns:* "Draw Thou My Soul, O Christ"; "What Grace, O Lord, and Beauty Shone"; (2) *Folk Hymns:* "There's a Quiet Understanding" *(Exodus Songbook)*; "We're Here to Be Happy" *(The Genesis Songbook)*; "They'll Know We Are Christians by Our Love" *(Songbook for Saints and Sinners, The Genesis Songbook,* and other collections); "Yahweh"; "Hosanna"; "O God Our Father" (all in *Wherever You Go)*; "Our Peace and Integrity" *(Listen)*.

Alternatives for the *second* hymn: (1) *Standard Hymns:* "O Master, Let Me Walk With Thee"; "Savior, Teach Me Day by Day"; "I Would Be True"; "We Give Thee But Thine Own". (2) *Folk Hymns:* "On Our Way"; "You Are the Salt of the Earth"; "Break Not the Circle" (both in *Exodus Songbook)*; "Thank You, Lord"; "Sing Love Songs" (both in *Avery and Marsh Songbook)*; "All I Ask of You" *(Listen)*; "I Believe in You" *(A New Commandment)*.

Movies. Use one of the following movies: (1) *Angel and Big Joe* (16mm, color, 27 minutes, produced by LCA). A film about the good influence that a telephone repairman has on a young boy. (2) *Luke Was There* (16mm, color, 32 minutes, produced by LCA). A film about how a perceptive counselor helps a young boy. For information on film rentals, see "Movies" in Part Three of this book.

Solo. Have a soloist sing "Song for a Friend" (in "Additional Hymns and Service Music" in Part Three of this book), or "Take All the Lost Home" *(A New Commandment)*.

ORDER OF WORSHIP

Call to Worship *(responsively)*

You are God's people! God calls you to love and care for one another!

We want to answer God's call! We want to be loving examples for all people!

Then let us worship God, so that we may discover how to demonstrate God's love in all that we do.

Hymn: "Lord, Speak to Me"

Prayer of Reflection *(unison)*

O God, you have given us a perfect example in Jesus the Christ. He accepted and loved people. He cared for the sick and the needy. He gave his life in service and sacrifice.

We want to be like Jesus. We want to love as he loved.

Give us wisdom and insight and courage, so that we may follow his example and thus be an example and a source of strength for others. Amen.

Offering and Doxology

Scripture: Matthew 18:6-7; 1 Corinthians 8:9-13; Matthew 5:19

Probe of the Word: How We Influence Other People

Characters for the role play are as follows: *Mr. In-Crowd*—a fellow who is the conformist *par excellence* (the right clothes, the right friends, up-to-date in musical tastes, and so forth); *Ms. Bad News*—the quintessential pessimist; *Mr. Frantic*—a "go-go" type who is always busy seeking pleasure; *Ms. Goodway*—a committed Christian; *Mr. Undecided*—just what the name says.

Introduce the characters, and begin the skit.

Mr. Undecided: *"What's the use? I don't know what to do with my life!"*

Mr. In-Crowd: *"Simple, man! Just do what everybody else does—wear the Nikes, wear the Izods, guzzle the booze, cruise with the in-crowd, stick with the status. . . ."*

Mr. Frantic: *"That sounds good to me! Just enjoy it! Live in the fast lane! Don't stop to think about life! Just keep a-moving"!"*

Mr. In-Crowd: *"Yeah! But don't lose your cool! Always make a good impression!"*

Ms. Bad News: *"Oh, yeah? I agree with ol' Undecided's first word. What's the use? You're gonna end up losing regardless of what you do. That's the way life is!"*

Ms. Goodway: *"Hold on! As a Christian, I believe there's a better way to live! You don't have to be with the in-crowd. You don't have to be on the go-go-go. You don't have to give in to all those pessimistic thoughts. Jesus says . . ."* . . .

Have the role play continued with all five role players participating in the discussion. Afterward, have a discussion of how the five players represent influences that participants come in contact with. Conclude by brainstorming some specific ways in which participants can be good influences upon other people.

Hymn: "Take My Life and Let It Be Consecrated"

Benediction *(to be said by the worship leader)*

Go forth into a world that can influence you in positive ways and negative ways! Make your influence count for good, through Jesus Christ our Lord and our example! Amen.

WORSHIP SERVICE NO. 26: "THE POWER OF PRAYER"

Guidelines for the Basic Service

Purpose: To help persons learn more about personal prayer during a worship service.

Resources and Materials Needed: Bibles; hymnals; paper and pencils; newsprint and markers, *or* chalkboard, chalk, and eraser

Hymns. The two suggested hymns are found in many hymnals. Alternative ideas are given in "Additional Ideas for This Service."

Offering and Doxology. This section is optional. For ideas on Doxologies, see "Additional Hymns and Service Music" in Part Three of this book.

Scripture. Matthew 6:5-15 and Matthew 7:7-11 present some of Jesus' teachings on prayer. The other two selections give examples of Jesus' own prayers—for himself (Matthew 26: 36-39) and for other people (John 17:6-21). The TEV is preferred for all selections except the Lord's Prayer (Matthew 6:9-13), for which the more familiar RSV is recommended.

Probe of the Word. This part of the service consists of three activities: (1) A Scripture Search on Prayer; (2) An Analysis of the Lord's Prayer; and (3) A Prayer Covenant Activity. Here are *suggested answers* for the first two activities: *Scripture Search: Matthew 6:5*—Don't try to impress people with your prayers. *Matthew 6:6*—Pray in solitude so God will hear you. *Matthew 6:7*—Don't use a lot of meaningless words. *Matthew 6:8*—Be assured that God knows your needs. *Matthew 7:7-11*—God loves you and will give you what is good for you. *Matthew 6:14-15*—Be in a state of love and forgiveness with others when you pray. *Matthew 26:36-39*—Pray for God's will to be done. *John 17:6-21*—Pray for other people as well as for yourself.
Analysis of the Lord's Prayer: Praise of God—verse 9; *Confession and Request for Forgiveness*—verse 12; *Petition*—verses 11 and 13 (also possible: verse 12); *Intercession*—verse 10.

Additional Ideas for This Service

If you have additional time and/or resources, you may wish to consider some of the following suggestions for alteration of the basic service:

Hymns. Substitute standard hymns or folk hymns for those suggested in the basic service. Alternatives for the *first* hymn: (1) *Standard Hymns:* "Jesus, Thy Boundless Love to Me"; "Breathe on Me, Breath of God"; "Spirit of God, Descend Upon My Heart"; "Guide Me, O Thou Great Jehovah"; (2) *Folk Hymns:* "Jesus, We Want to Meet" (*Songbook for Saints and Sinners*); "Psalm of Thanksgiving" (*Exodus Songbook*); "In Him We Live" (*Abba, Father*).
Alternatives for the *second* hymn: (1) *Standard Hymns:* "Take Time to Be Holy"; "I Need Thee Every Hour"; "Lead, Kindly Light"; "Master, Speak! Thy Servant Heareth"; "Prayer Is the Soul's Sincere Desire"; (2) *Folk Hymns:* "Day by Day" (*The Genesis Songbook*); "It's Me, O Lord" (*Songbook for Saints and Sinners*); "When I'm Feeling Lonely" (*Avery and Marsh Songbook*).

The Lord's Prayer. Have the group or a soloist sing the Lord's Prayer. See the versions found in *The Genesis Songbook, Exodus Songbook,* and "Additional Hymns and Service Music" in Part Three of this book. For a special version with new and intriguing words, use Joe Wise's *Our Father* (in the songbook *Pockets*).

Audio-Visual Resource. Use the audio-visual kit *Teach Us to Pray* as part of the Probe of the Word. This kit includes a soundsheet and a film strip. For information on ordering this kit, contact Cokesbury at one of the addresses given in the note on hymnals, Part One of this book.

ORDER OF WORSHIP

Call to Worship *(to be said by the worship leader)*

God is everywhere! God is in the infinite galaxies of space and in every place on earth! God is in this service of worship, and God is in our hearts! Let us worship God together, so that we may learn how to talk with God.

Hymn: "Jesus, My Strength, My Hope"

Prayer of Reflection *(unison)*

O God, once again we present our prayers to you. We come into your presence with our words of praise. We approach you with our confessions of failure and our requests for forgiveness. We talk with you about our needs and the needs of our neighbors. We ask you to bless us and our families and friends.

O God, accept our prayers, even though they are imperfect and incomplete. Teach us how to pray, so that our prayer life may be focused on you. Show us how to share our deepest thoughts and feelings—both in our prayers and in our lives, through Jesus Christ who taught us about praying and living. Amen.

Offering and Doxology

Scripture: Matthew 6:5-15; 7:7-11

Probe of the Word: Improving My Personal Prayer Life

A Scripture Search on Prayer. Divide the group into teams of two or three persons. Give each person a pencil and at least three sheets of paper. Have the teams read the following Scriptural selections and write out at least one prayer guideline suggested by each selection: (1) Matthew 6:5; (2) Matthew 6:6; (3) Matthew 6:7; (4) Matthew 6:8; (5) Matthew 7:7-11; (6) Matthew 6:14-15; (7) Matthew 26:36-39; (8) John 17:6-21. Afterward, collate and discuss responses. Be open to valid interpretation that may differ from those suggested in "Guidelines for the Basic Service."

An Analysis of the Lord's Prayer. Again divide into teams. Have the teams choose verses from Matthew 6:9-13 that are examples of each of the following: (1) Praise of God; (2) Confession and Request for Forgiveness; (3) Petition (prayer for one's own needs); (4) Intercession (prayer for other people—in this case, a request for God's will to be done in the world). After all teams have finished, collate and discuss responses. Again, be open to valid interpretations that may differ from those suggested in "Guidelines for the Basic Service."

A Prayer Covenant Activity. Have persons work individually to write out prayer covenants for the coming week. Suggestions for items to include: (1) A Daily Time When I Will Pray; (2) The Place Where I Will Pray; (3) Things I Will Praise and Thank God For; (4) Things I Will Confess and Ask Forgiveness For; (5) Some Requests I Will Make for Myself; (6) Some Requests I Will Make for Other Persons.

Afterward, have voluntary sharing. Then tell participants to take their covenants home and use them as guides for prayer during the coming week.

Hymn: "Open My Eyes, That I May See"

Concluding Prayer: The Lord's Prayer *(unison)*

WORSHIP SERVICE NO. 27: "REPENTING"
(Easter Season)

Guidelines for the Basic Service

Purpose: To give persons an opportunity to experience repentance and forgiveness in a worship service.

Resources and Materials Needed: Bibles; hymnals; a pencil and a piece of paper for each participant; a trash can or a fireproof container; matches (optional)

Hymns. The two suggested hymns are found in many hymnals. Alternative ideas are given in "Additional Ideas for This Service."

Offering and Doxology. This section is optional, but it is preferable that it be included—since an offering is always an appropriate response for people who have received the gift of forgiveness. For ideas on Doxologies, see "Additional Hymns and Service Music" in Part Three of this book.

Scripture. Psalms 51 is the classic Biblical prayer of repentance. It expresses both remorse for sin and an assurance of God's forgiveness. The passage from First John states the Christian's assurance that God will forgive those who are sorry for their sins.

Probe of the Word. If you decide to burn the pieces of paper used in this activity, be sure to take all necessary precautions. It would be good to have **a fire extinguisher on hand!**

Additional Ideas for This Service

If you have additional time and/or resources, you may wish to consider some of the following suggestions for alteration of the basic service:

Hymns. Substitute standard hymns or folk hymns for those suggested in the basic service. Alternatives for the *first* hymn: (1) *Standard Hymns:* "Guide Me, O Thou Great Jehovah"; "Jesus, Thine All-Victorious Love"; "Lord, I Want to Be a Christian"; "We Are Climbing Jacob's Ladder"; (2) *Folk Hymns:* "Jesus Is Life" *(Abba, Father)*; "I Lift Up My Eyes" *(Songbook for Saints and Sinners)*.

Alternatives for the *second* hymn: (1) *Standard Hymns:* "Spirit of God, Descend Upon My Heart"; "My Faith Looks Up to Thee"; "I Heard the Voice of Jesus Say"; "Savior, Like a Shepherd Lead Us"; "O Come and Dwell in Me"; "Amazing Grace"; (2) *Folk Hymns:* "When You Least Expect Him"; "When I'm Feeling Lonely"; "Thank You, Lord"; "Every Morning Is Easter Morning" (all in *Avery and Marsh Songbook*); "Morning Has Broken" *(Genesis Songbook)*; "Joy Is Like the Rain" *(Joy Is Like the Rain)*; "Life Is the Answer *(Show Me Your Smile)*; "Dance in the Darkness" *(Abba, Father)*; "New Life, New Creation" *(Listen)*; "Happiness"; "Anything Happens" (both in *Wherever You Go*).

Words of Hope. Substitute a folk hymn for the scriptural words. Possibilities: "I'm OK, You're OK"; "New World Coming"; "You've Got a Friend" (all in *Exodus Songbook*). Another alternative: Use James Taylor's recording of Carole King's "You've Got a Friend" (from his Warner album *Greatest Hits*).

Call to Confession. Just before participants pray the Prayer of Confession, play Paul Simon's recording of "Some Folks' Lives Roll Easy" (from his Columbia album *Still Crazy After All These Years*).

Movie. Show the movie *The Way Home* (16mm, color, 15 minutes, produced by TeleKETICS) just prior to the Probe of the Word. This movie is a modern retelling of the story of the Prodigal Son. For information on film rentals, see "Movies" in Part Three of this book.

ORDER OF WORSHIP

Call to Worship *(responsively)*

Let us renew our relationship with God.

We hope to find a new relationship and new life.

In order to make that discovery, we must be honest about our sinfulness.

We are ready to be honest. We are ready to hear God's word.

Then listen and be joyful! Through hearing and responding to God's word, we can find forgiveness and acceptance and a new self—with new possibilities.

In the spirit of this search, we will worship together. Amen.

Hymn: "Love Divine, All Loves Excelling"

Scripture from the Old Testament: Psalms 51:1-4, 6-12, 16-17

Prayer of Confession *(unison)*

O God, sometimes we don't understand why we speak and act as we do. Sometimes our behavior baffles us. Like Saint Paul, we would say: "I do not understand what I do; for I don't do what I would like to do, but instead I do what I hate."

Sometimes we feel that we are controlled by unseen forces that cause us to be less than we want to be, that compel us to say unkind words and act in hurtful, harmful ways. We speak and act thoughtlessly, and later we feel sorry because of the damage we have done, the hurt we have caused.

Help us to know that, whatever we have said or done, we can be accepted and forgiven. Help us to realize that through your love and your grace we can change. Help us to begin to change today—at this moment, through the power of Jesus Christ, our Lord. Amen.

Words of Hope from the New Testament: 1 John 1:5-9

Probe of the Word: Repenting

Give each person a pencil and a piece of paper. Tell the group that this activity will be done *in strictest confidence.* Then ask everyone to write on his or her piece of paper a sinful thought, statement, or action that he or she feels sorry for having committed. Then have each person fold his or her piece of paper and give it to you.

Tear the pieces of paper into small shreds and place them in a trash can or a fireproof container. Burn the pieces—if you have chosen to do so. (If you do not burn them, make sure that they are completely disposed of afterward.)

Then say: *The Bible tells us that if we are sorry for our sins and promise to try to live better in the future, God will forgive our sins. They will be as powerless as these shreds of paper. The Old Testament word for "repentance" means: "to go in a new direction." The New Testament word means: "to get a new frame of mind." As we put these sins behind us and accept God's forgiveness, let us change the direction of our lives and let us get a new outlook on life!*

Hymn: "Breathe on Me, Breath of God"

Benediction *(to be said by the worship leader)*

You are forgiven and accepted by God! Go to be God's people in the world! Amen.

WORSHIP SERVICE NO. 28: "HELPING THE HUNGRY"
(Easter Season)

Guidelines for the Basic Service

Purpose: To give persons an opportunity to participate in a worship service in which they become more aware of the needs of the hungry and ways to help the hungry.

Resources and Materials Needed: Bibles; hymnals; food and beverage items; "play money"; paper and pencils (optional); offering plate(s) (optional)

Hymns. The two suggested hymns are found in many hymnals. Alternative ideas are given in "Additional Ideas for This Service."

Offering and Doxology. This section is optional, but it is recommended that it be included. For ideas on Doxologies, see "Additional Hymns and Service Music" in Part Three of this book.

Scripture. In Isaiah 58:1-7, God tells the people of Israel that their fasting is useless unless they help the oppressed, the hungry, the homeless, and the poor. Matthew 25:31-40 is part of Jesus' Parable of the Last Judgment, in which he points out that we serve him by helping needy persons—those who are lonely, imprisoned, sick; those who are in need of food and clothing. The TEV is the preferred version.

Probe of the Word. The main activity consists of a simulation game designed to help participants discover how it feels to have very little to eat while others have plenty. In preparation for this activity, make play money ("Lukers") in these denominations: 1 Luker, 5 Lukers, 10 Lukers, 20 Lukers, 100 Lukers. You will also need to secure food and beverage items in these two categories: (1) delicious "goodies"; and (2) plain foodstuffs. Suggestions of foods and drinks are given in the probe itself.

Additional Ideas for This Service

Hymns. Substitute standard hymns or folk hymns for those suggested in the basic service. Alternatives for the *first* hymn: (1) *Standard Hymns:* "Lord, Speak to Me"; "O Son of Man, Thou Madest Known"; (2) *Folk Hymns:* "They'll Know We Are Christians by Our Love" (*Songbook for Saints and Sinners, The Genesis Songbook,* and other collections); "Come Praise, Alleluia" (*Songbook for Saints and Sinners*).

Alternatives for the *second* hymn: (1) *Standard Hymn:* "The Voice of God Is Calling"—change "men" to "all"; (2) *Folk Hymns:* "The Spirit of the Lord" ("Additional Hymns and Service Music" in Part Three of this book); "Choose Life" (*The Genesis Songbook*); "Shared Bread" (*Songbook for Saints and Sinners*); "Love Is Here"—omit stanza 3 (*Locusts and Wild Honey*).

Movies. Use one of the following movies: (1) *The Longest Stride* (16mm, color, 15 minutes, produced by Furman S. Baldwin). A film about what it's like to live on $100 a year. (2) *Because They Care* (16mm, color, 30 minutes, produced by CBS). A film about Church World Service's CROP program to help the hungry. (3) *Diet for a Small Planet* (16mm, color, 30 minutes, produced by Bullfrog Films). A film about helping the hungry by being sensible about diet. (4) *Hunger* (16mm, color, 12 minutes, produced by National Film Board of Canada). An animated allegory about a man whose greed causes him to swell up to huge proportions.

For information on film rentals, see "Movies" in Part Three of this book.

Resources. If you would like to secure copies of *Alternative Celebrations Catalogue* or other resources on responsible life-styles, contact the Alternative Resources Center, 1124 Main St., P.O. Box 1707, Forest Park, GA 30051 (404-361-5823).

ORDER OF WORSHIP

Call to Worship *(responsively)*
You are God's people! God calls you to help those who are hungry!
We want to respond to this call!
Then let us worship together, so that God will show us how to share with the hungry people of the world.

Hymn: "What Shall I Render to My God"

Prayer of Confession *(unison)*
O God, we thank you that we can eat when we are hungry. Our tables are filled with tasty foods. We feast on burgers and fries at fast-food chains. We devour delicious dinners at fancy restaurants. Our stomachs are often stuffed to the limit.

We confess that we have not always been aware of those whose stomachs and lives are empty. We have not done all that we could to help the hungry. We have not responded as we should to the needs of the poor.

O God, make us keenly aware of those who do not have enough to eat. Help us to change our living habits and our giving habits, so that we may help the hungry people of the world. Amen.

Words of Forgiveness and Hope *(to be said by the worship leader)*
You are forgiven and accepted! Now change your ways and your words, your minds and your meals—so that you can reach out to feed those who are famished!

Scripture: Isaiah 58:1-7, Matthew 25:31-40

Probe of the Word: The Wide World Foodway Store
Divide the group into two sub-groups: the affluent people (a minority of the group); and the poor people (the majority of the group). Give each affluent person 125 Lukers and each poor person 11 Lukers. Then have persons make their purchases and sit down for a meal together.

Have on hand enough food and beverages so that each affluent person will be able to buy several treats and a beverage and each poor person will be able to buy some of the plain foods and some water. Have the items priced as follows: *Items at 50 Lukers each:* Can of Soda; Glass of Milk; Piece of Cake; Candy Bar; *Items at 25 Lukers each:* Cookie; Piece of Fruit; Small Box of Raisins; Small Bag of Potato Chips; *Items at 10 Lukers each:* Saltine Cracker; Piece of Sliced Bread; *Items at 5 Lukers each;* One Potato Chip; One Piece of Popcorn; *Item at 1 Luker each:* Glass of Water.

Process the experience by discussing feelings and thoughts that the participants had during the activity. Give special attention to how members of each group felt about persons in the other group. Conclude by brainstorming ideas on ways to help the hungry. Make action plans for carrying out some of the ideas.

Prepare participants for the offering by suggesting that they give money or pledges of money to be sent to a denominational agency or some other organization involved in helping hungry people.

Offering and Doxology

Hymn: "O Thou Who Art the Shepherd"

Benediction *(to be said by the worship leader)*
Go forth to feed the hungry! Change your diets and your lives! Share your good gifts with those who are in need! Amen.

WORSHIP SERVICE NO. 29: "THE SPIRIT OF THE LORD"
(Easter Season)

Guidelines for the Basic Service

Purpose: To give persons an opportunity to participate in a worship service in which they learn more about the Holy Spirit.

Resources and Materials Needed: Bibles; hymnals; pencils and paper; newsprint and markers, *or* chalkboard, chalk, and eraser; Bible commentaries; dictionaries

Hymns. The two suggested hymns are found in many hymnals. Alternative ideas are given in "Additional Ideas for This Service."

Offering and Doxology. This section is optional. For ideas on Doxologies, see "Additional Hymns and Service Music" in Part Three of this book.

Scripture. This service utilizes many Scriptural selections dealing with the Spirit. Ideas for their usage are given in the Probe of the Word. For more information on these passages, consult some good Bible commentaries. If you do not own commentaries, borrow them from your pastor, your church library, or some other library.

Probe of the Word. This part of the service is a directed Bible study. You should have Bible commentaries and dictionaries available for participants to refer to.

Additional Ideas for This Service

If you have additional time and/or resources, you may wish to consider some of the following suggestions for alteration of the basic service:

Hymns. Substitute standard hymns or folk hymns for those suggested in the basic service. (1) *Standard Hymns:* Alternatives for either the *first* hymn or the *second* hymn: "Come, Holy Spirit, Heavenly Daove"; "Breathe on Me, Breath of God"; "Holy Spirit, Truth Divine"; "Spirit of God, Descend Upon My Heart"; "Spirit Divine, Attend Our Prayers".

(2) *Folk Hymns:* Alternatives for the *first* hymn: "Canticle for Pentecost" *(The Genesis Songbook)*; "The Spirit of the Lord" ("Additional Hymns and Service Music" in Part Three of this book); "Spirit of God" *(Joy Is Like the Rain)*; Alternatives for the *second* hymn: "Come, Share the Spirit" *(Exodus Songbook)*; "Our Peace and Integrity"; "New Life, New Creation" (both in *Listen*); "If There Is a Holy Spirit" *(Songbook for Saints and Sinners, Avery and Marsh Songbook)*; "The Church Within Us" *(Songbook for Saints and Sinners)*; "A Song of the Spirit" ("Additional Hymns and Service Music" in Part Three of this book).

Movies. Use one of the following movies: (1) *One Who Was There* (16mm, color, 37 minutes, produced by United Methodist Communications). A film about a woman, a friend of Jesus, who finds her faith renewed thirty years after his death by her encounter with a spirit-filled group of new believers. (2) *The Parable* (16mm, color, 22 minutes). An allegorical film that shows how the spirit of a murdered clown (a Christ figure) is reborn in the life of the man who killed him.

Recorded Music. Use recorded music for a prelude, offertory, and/or postlude. Suggestions: "Beautiful Vision" from Van Morrison's Warner Records album *Beautiful Vision*; "I'll Find My Way Home" from John and Vangelis' Polydor album *The Friends of Mr. Cairo* (*Note:* This song appears *only* on the *brown-cover* version of the album, not on the white-cover version).

ORDER OF WORSHIP

Call to Worship *(responsively)*
The Spirit of the Lord is upon you, for you are God's people!
We want to feel God's Spirit moving in our lives!
Then let us worship God in spirit and in truth, so that we may be inspired by God's Holy Spirit.

Hymn: "Come, Holy Ghost, Our Heart Inspire"

Prayer of Reflection *(unison)*
O God, we want to feel the impact of your power upon our lives. We want to respond to your life-giving Spirit.
Come like a mighty wind and invade the vacuums of our lives. Rush in like a roaring fire and burn away our unbelief. Shout to us in a loud voice and shatter the silence of our souls.
Fill us with the force of your Spirit, so we may fearlessly speak your word and follow your will for our lives. Amen.

Scripture: Luke 4:16-22

Probe of the Word: Understanding Biblical Teachings About the Holy Spirit
Divide the group into five teams for the directed Bible study. As an alternative, you may have the whole group work on the five assignments in sequence. Give each person a pencil and a piece of paper. Then have the teams (or the whole group) read the Biblical selections in each category and do the assignments. Inform the participants that commentaries and dictionaries may be used. The selections and assignments are as follows:
(1) The Spirit in the Old Testament: Genesis 1:1-5; I Samuel 10:1-6; Exra 1:1-5; Ezekiel 11:24-25 (RSV). List several things that the Spirit does or causes.
(2) The Spirit in Jesus' Life: Luke 4:16-21 (TEV). List the things that the Spirit causes Jesus to do.
(3) The Promise of the Holy Spirit: John 14:15-20 (TEV). Tell how Jesus says the Holy Spirit will work in the lives of his followers.
(4) The Gifts of the Spirit: 1 Corinthians 12:4-11; Galatians 5:16-23 (RSV). List and explain the gifts of the Spirit.
(5) The Test of the Spirit's Presence: 1 John 4:1-4 (RSV). Describe how people will be able to tell the difference between the work of the true Spirit and the work of false spirits.
After all assignments have been completed, collate and discuss responses. Talk about ways in which persons can get in touch with the Spirit in their lives. Give special attention to the disciplines of Scripture reading, prayer, and meditation.

Offering and Doxology

Hymn: "Spirit of Life, in This New Dawn"

Benediction *(to be said by the worship leader)*
God's Spirit is in your midst! You can be Spirit-filled people! Go forth from this place and let the Spirit speak to you, so that you may be anointed to do God's work in the world! Amen.

WORSHIP SERVICE NO. 30: "THE TIME OF OUR LIVES"
(Easter Season)

Guidelines for the Basic Service

Purpose: To give persons an opportunity to participate in a worship service in which they learn how to be better stewards of their time.

Resources and Materials Needed: Bibles; hymnals; pencils and paper; sheets with blank "time pies" (optional—see below)

Hymns. The two suggested hymns are found in many hymnals. Alternative ideas are given in "Additional Ideas for This Service."

Offering and Doxology. This section is optional. For ideas on Doxologies, see "Additional Hymns and Service Music" in Part Three of this book.

Scripture. Ecclesiastes 3:1-8 points out that in God's plan there is a proper time for everything. The selections from John's Gospel (7:6-8; 13:1; 17:1) show Jesus' emphasis on taking decisive action at the right time—the time that God chooses. The TEV is preferred for the selections.

Probe of the Word. This part of the service is designed to give participants an opportunity to analyze their usage of time and to make plans for using time better. The main activity involves filling in two weekly "time pies"—one to show the person's present pattern of time usage and one to show a plan for future time usage. For a sample of how these two pies might look, see the illustration in the worship service.

To create the blank pies for the service, you may wish to draw two circles on a sheet of paper, label one of the circles "My Present Weekly Time Pie" and the other "My Ideal Weekly Time Pie," and then make photocopies for all participants; or you may choose to give participants blank sheets and have them construct the blank pies.

Additional Ideas for This Service

If you have additional time and/or resources, you may wish to consider some of the following suggestions for alteration of the basic service:

Hymns. Substitute standard hymns or folk hymns for those suggested in the basic service. Alternatives for the *first* hymn: (1) *Standard Hymns:* "Sing to the Great Jehovah's Praise"; "Praise to the Living God"; "O God, Our Help in Ages Past"; (2) *Folk Hymns:* "In Him We Live" (*Abba, Father*); "God Is Working His Purposes Out" (*Songbook for Saints and Sinners*); "Morning Has Broken" (*The Genesis Songbook*).

Alternatives for the *second* hymn: (1) *Standard Hymns:* "Forth Every Morning in Thy Name"; "New Every Morning Is the Love"; (2) *Folk Hymns:* "Day by Day"; "Genesis One"; "Turn! Turn! Turn!" (all in *The Genesis Songbook*); "Moments to Live By" *(Listen)*; "Happiness" *(Wherever You Go)*.

Movies. Use one of the following movies: (1) *Time Structures* (16mm, color, 30 minutes, produced by United Methodist Communications). A film that shows the relation between time usage and priorities. (2) *Leisure* (16mm, color, 14 minutes, produced by Bruce Petty Films). An animated film that gives a light-hearted history of the "art" of leisure.

For information on film rentals, see "Movies" in Part Three of this book.

Solo. Have a soloist sing "Somewhere" *(Exodus Songbook)*.

Recorded Music. Use recorded music for a prelude, offertory, and/or postlude. Suggestions: "Time in a Bottle" from Jim Croce's ABC album *Photographs and Memories*; "Wasted on the Way" from Crosby, Stills, and Nash's Atlantic album *Daylight Again*; "Forever Young" from Joan Baez' A&M album *From Every Stage*.

ORDER OF WORSHIP

Call to Worship *(to be said by the worship leader)*
God has given you the gift of time! God has also given you the freedom to use your time as you choose!
Let us worship God together and learn God's lessons about time, so that we may be responsible in the ways we use the moments of our lives.

Hymn: "God of Our Life"

Prayer of Reflection *(unison)*
O God, we live in a world that is caught up in the tides of time. Even as we speak, the stream of time flows on through channels of change and challenge. Even as we wait in this hour, the massive river of time rushes on—making the moments of our lives ever new and ever different.

Make us conscious of the course of our lives. Show us how to plan and prepare, so that time will not toss us about in its tides. Give us wisdom and insight, so that we may determine the direction of our journey and find your will in the miracle of our moments. Amen.

Offering and Doxology

Scripture: Ecclesiastes 3:1-8; John 7:6-8; 13:1; 17:1

Probe of the Word: A Look at My Use of Time
Hand out pencils and sheets of paper (or photocopied sheets with the blank "time pies"). Have participants work individually to fill in their present weekly "time pies." You may use the sample pie on the left below as an example:

My Present Weekly Time Pie   **My Ideal Weekly Time Pie**

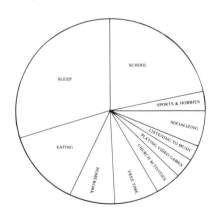
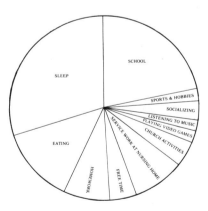

Afterward, have voluntary sharing. Then talk about the ideas in the Scriptures—especially Jesus' determination to use his time according to God's will. Have participants talk about their priorities for their lives and how these priorities might affect their use of time. Then have them fill in the ideal weekly "pies." You may use the sample "pie" on the right above as an example.

After all have finished this activity, have another period of voluntary sharing. Give particular attention to changes in the "pies" and reasons for the changes.

Hymn: "Take Time to Be Holy"

Benediction *(to be said by the worship leader)*
Go forth to live in a world that is bounded by time! Pray to God that time will not be your prison, but rather an open door that leads to days and years of living according to God's purposes! Amen.

WORSHIP SERVICE NO. 31: "FORGIVING OTHERS"
(Easter Season)

Guidelines for the Basic Service

Purpose: To give persons an opportunity to participate in a worship service that helps them learn about forgiving other people.

Resources and Materials Needed: Bibles; hymnals; an altar; rocks (one for each participant; size—at least as large as a piece of coarse gravel)

Hymns. The two suggested hymns are found in many hymnals. Alternative ideas are given in "Additional Ideas for This Service."

Offering and Doxology. This section is optional, but it is preferable that it be included—since an offering is always an appropriate response for people who have received the gift of forgiveness. For ideas on Doxologies, see "Additional Hymns and Service Music" in Part Three of this book.

Scripture. John 7:53-8:11 is the story of the woman caught in the act of adultery. In this story, Jesus teaches that we are not to be judgmental toward other people. The climactic point in the story occurs when Jesus points out that all people are sinful and thus have no grounds for condemning others. The stone that had been a symbol of judgment becomes—when laid aside—a symbol of understanding and forgiveness. Recommended versions: TEV or RSV.
Matthew 6:12-15 teaches that God forgives those who forgive others. The TEV is preferred.

Probe of the Word. It is suggested that the rocks used in this activity be returned to participants and taken home as reminders of God's forgiving love. If you choose not to return the rocks, omit the second paragraph of the benediction.

Additional Ideas for This Service

If you have additional time and/or resources, you may wish to consider some of the following suggestions for alteration of the basic service:

Hymns. Substitute folk hymns for the hymns suggested in the basic service. Alternatives for the *first* hymn: "New Circles" (music in "Additional Hymns and Service Music" in Part Three of this book); "What the World Needs Now Is Love" *(Exodus Songbook)*; "Love One Another"; "Magic Penny" (both in *Exodus Songbook*).
Alternatives for the *second* hymn: "Thanks Be to God" *(Songbook for Saints and Sinners)*; "Thank You, Lord" *(Avery and Marsh Songbook)*; "Anything Happens" *(Wherever You Go)*; "New Life, New Creation" *(Listen)*.

The Lord's Prayer. Sing the Lord's Prayer or have a soloist sing it. Possible versions: the version in "Additional Hymns and Service Music" in Part Three of this book; Sister Janet Mead's version in *Exodus Songbook*.

Recorded Music. Use John Denver's song "Opposite Tables" (from his RCA album *Seasons of the Heart*) as a Prayer of Confession immediately before the Probe of the Word. Coordinate slides with the song to make an audio-visual presentation. For ideas on making home-made slides and producing slide-and-music presentations, see pages 116-126 of *Youth Workers' Handbook* (C-4 Resources, 1983) or refer to some of the books on audio-visual techniques listed in Part Three of this book.

ORDER OF WORSHIP

Call to Worship *(responsively)*
We are here to worship God. We gather as human beings who are created in the image of God.
For that reason, we have fantastic potential! We can do great things!
Our God is a loving and forgiving God. As people created in God's image, we should be able to love and forgive other people.
Sometimes we don't live up to that potential! We find it hard to forgive someone who has hurt us. It's easier just to hold a grudge!
Jesus said that we should pray: "Forgive us our trespasses as we forgive those who trespass against us." As we worship God, let us try to learn how to forgive in the same way that God forgives.
We will try to learn that lesson! We will try to discover the power of forgiveness!

Hymn: "Amazing Grace"

Scripture: John 7:53-8:11

Probe of the Word: A Symbol of Forgiveness
Give everyone a rock. Ask each person to think about someone who has wronged him or her through some hurtful word or action. Then have everyone concentrate on the rock that he or she is holding. Talk about the hardness of the rock and about how the rock could be thrown at someone. Ask each person to think about the feelings that he or she feels toward the person who is responsible for the hurtful word or action. Then read John 8:7 again. Next pray these words: *O God, forgive us our trespasses as we forgive those who trespass against us.* Then ask everyone to place his or her rock on the altar. Pray: *O God, as we leave these rocks on your altar, may we also leave there any hard feelings or anger that we have felt toward those who have wronged us. Forgive us, and help us to forgive others. Amen.*

Scripture: Matthew 6:14-15

Offering and Doxology

The Lord's Prayer *(unison)*

Hymn: "Now Thank We All Our God"

Benediction *(to be said by the worship leader while handing out the rocks)*
Go into the world as forgiven people. Take the love and forgiveness of God into all your relationships. . . .
These rocks are symbols of the fact that we all stand in need of forgiveness from God and from one another. Take one of these rocks with you as a reminder that forgiven people must forgive others. . . .
May God's blessing and strength go with you, through Jesus Christ our Lord. Amen.

WORSHIP SERVICE NO. 32: "OUR LEADER TRIUMPHANT"
(Palm Sunday)

Guidelines for the Basic Service

Purpose: To give persons an opportunity to re-enact the events of Palm Sunday during a worship service.

Resources and Materials Needed: Bibles; hymnals; placards, signs, and/or banners

Hymns. The two suggested hymns are found in many hymnals. Alternative ideas are given in "Additional Ideas for This Service."

Offering and Doxology. This section is optional. For ideas on Doxologies, see "Additional Hymns and Service Music" in Part Three of this book.

Scripture. Mark 11:1-10 tells the story of Jesus' triumphant entry into Jerusalem on Palm Sunday. The narratives in Mark 11:15-18 and 12:37*b*-40 tell of two incidents when Jesus criticizes the Temple merchants and the religious leaders. The TEV is preferred for all selections.

Probe of the Word. This part of the service consists mainly of a mini-skit based on the Palm Sunday events. Choose persons to play the parts of "Josh Crissom" (or "Jessie Crissom")—the Jesus character—and the "cheerleaders." The person who plays Josh (or Jessie) should be dramatically-inclined and able to ad-lib. You may wish to use a non-member for this part. If you choose an outside person, make sure that he or she is not an "authority figure" who might intimidate members of your group. The "cheerleaders" should carry placards, signs, banners, and so forth, with slogans like: "We love Josh (or Jessie)"; "Hurray for J.C."; "Josh (or Jessie) Crissom Should Be Our Leader."

Contact the players in advance and spend some time coaching them in their roles. A full-scale rehearsal is recommended.

Additional Ideas for This Service

If you have additional time and/or resources, you may wish to consider some of the following ideas for alteration of the basic service:

Hymns. Substitute standard hymns or folk hymns for those suggested in the basic service. Any of the following hymns may be substituted for either of the suggested hymns: (1) *Standard Hymns:* "So Lowly Doth the Savior Ride"; "Hosanna, Loud Hosanna"; (2) *Folk Hymns:* "Here He Comes"; "Hosanna, Hallelujah" (both in *Avery and Marsh Songbook*); "You Can Tell the World" *(The Genesis Songbook)*; "Jesus Is Life" *(Abba, Father)*; "Come, Praise Alleluia" *(Songbook for Saints and Sinners)*.

Movies. Use one the following movies: (1) *Jerusalem* (16mm, color, 18 minutes, The New Media Bible Series, produced by the Genesis Project). A film that tells the story of Jesus' Palm Sunday entry into Jerusalem and his anger at the market-like atmosphere of the Temple. (2) *Triumph and Defeat* (16mm, color or b/w, 30 minutes, The Living Christ Series, produced by Cathedral Films). A film that tells the story of Jesus' entry into Jerusalem, his cleansing of the Temple, and other events leading up to his trial.

For information on film rentals, see "Movies" in Part Three of this book.

Recorded Music. Use "Hosanna" from the MCA album *Jesus Christ Superstar* during the entrance of "Josh" (or "Jessie") in the Probe of the Word.

ORDER OF WORSHIP

Call to Worship *(to be said by the worship leader)*

Today is Palm Sunday! Let us worship God! Let us praise Jesus the Christ!

Hymn: "All Glory, Laud, and Honor"

Prayer of Reflection *(unison)*

O God, today we come into your presence with prayers of praise and hymns of happiness. We sing and rejoice because of Jesus our Lord. We join our voices with those who long ago applauded his approach. We echo their shouts of joy!

O God, as we sing out our praises on this Sunday of Palms, make us remember the other events of that day. As Jesus exposed the false religion of his day, may his Spirit uncover all that is false in us—so that we may be set free to serve you and others in the Spirit of Christ. Amen.

Offering and Doxology

Scripture: Mark 11:1-10, 15-18; 12:37*b*-40

Probe of the Word: Palm Sunday Revisited

As soon as the Scripture reading is finished, the "cheerleaders" are to open the door and bound into the room. They are to wave their placards, signs, and banners around and shout out their praises of Josh (or Jessie) Crissom. When Josh (or Jessie) comes through the door, they are to lead the group in wild applause and one of the following cheers: *"Joshua Crissom!/We'd love to kiss 'im!/He's the one who really cares!/He's the answer to our prayers!"* or *"Jessie, Jessie, Hip, Hooray!/She has come to save the day!/She's the one! We really need 'er!/She can be a super leader!"* Then the cheerleaders are to lead another round of applause.

Josh (or Jessie) then speaks to the group: *"I am here to tell you how you can become a super youth group—even better than you are now!* (applause) *With old Josh [or Jessie] advising you, you're gonna do great things!"* (applause) . . .

"But first . . . you have to take an honest look at yourselves. . . . (slight applause) *You're not perfect, you know! . . .* (no applause) *In fact, you've got a lot of problems! . . .* (groans from cheerleaders, who lead others in groaning) *Well, actually, you're in bad shape! . . .* (louder groans) *You're really a pretty useless group! . . .* (boos) *You spend most of your time on fund-raising [or recreation or some other aspect] and don't work at being the people of God!* (interrupted by loud boos) *You don't think so? You don't agree with me? Well, I'm gonna ask you some questions. . . ."* [Here the dialogue begins, with Josh (or Jessie) asking the group pointed questions about their purpose, their activites, and so forth].

After a few minutes of dialogue, discuss the activity. Give particular attention to how it relates to the Palm Sunday Scriptures. Help participants to see that honest self-examination is necessary if one is to experience the joys of Christian living.

Hymn: "Ride On, Ride On in Majesty"

Benediction *(to be said by the worship leader)*

Go forth to celebrate the Palm Sunday victory—the new life that is found through honestly facing who we are and what we can be! Amen.

WORSHIP SERVICE NO. 33: "CHRIST IS RISEN"
(Easter Sunday)

Guidelines for the Basic Service

Purpose: To give persons an opportunity to celebrate the joy of Easter in a worship service.

Resources and Materials Needed: Bibles; hymnals; decorations: cross and a black cloth; flowers; Easter banners and posters; balloons; and so forth

Hymns. The two suggested hymns are found in many hymnals. Alternative ideas are given in "Additional Ideas for This Service."

Gloria Patri. Musical settings for the Gloria Patri are found in many hymnals. See also "Additional Hymns and Service Music" in Part Three of this book.

Offering and Doxology. This section is optional, but it is recommended that it be included. For other ideas on Doxologies, see "Additional Hymns and Service Music" in Part Three of this book.

Scripture. Mark 15:37, 40-47 is to be used as the prologue to the service. The passage tells of Jesus' death and burial and the sadness of his disciples. Mark 16:1-7 is one of the accounts of the Resurrection. Matthew 28:16-20, Jesus' "great commission" to his disciples, is used as the benediction for the service. The TEV is preferred for all selections.

Probe of the Word. Part one of this probe is designed to give worshipers a feeling of exhilaration and excitement as the undecorated worship place is transformed by the addition of flowers, banners, and other decorations. Begin the service with the room bare except for a cross draped in a black cloth. After the call to worship, have everyone participate in the decoration of the room. Later, during Part Two of the probe, there will be an opportunity for persons to process their thoughts and feelings about the transformation.

Additional Ideas for This Service

Hymns. Substitute standard hymns or folk hymns for those suggested in the basic service. Any of the following hymns may be substituted for either of the suggested hymns: (1) *Standard Hymns:* Any of the hymns in the Easter section of your hymnal; (2) *Folk Hymns:* "Jesus Is Life" *(Abba, Father)*; "Lord of the Dance" *(The Genesis Songbook, Songbook for Saints and Sinners,* and other collections); "Alle, Alle"; "Crown Him With Many Crowns" *(Songbook for Saints and Sinners)*; "Easter Means There's Nothing Left to Fear"; "Love Come A-Tricklin' Down" "Allelu"—change "man" to "us" (all in *The Genesis Songbook)*; "Christ the Lord Is Risen"; "Every Morning Is Easter Morning" *(Avery and Marsh Songbook)*; "The Dawn Has Come" *(Listen)*.

Special Music. Have a trio sing "Mary's Song" *(Listen)*.

Movies. Use one of the following movies: (1) *That's Life* (16mm, color, 8 minutes, produced by Faith and Fantasy, Inc.). An allegorical film about a man who is "resurrected" as a clown. (2) *The Parable* (16mm, color, 22 minutes). An allegorical film about a murdered clown (a Christ figure) who is "resurrected" in the life of the man who killed him.

For information on film rentals, see "Movies" in Part Three of this book.

Audio-Visual Presentation. An interesting audio-visual allegory about Jesus can be created by showing the tennis-ball sequence from Saul Bass' film *Why Man Creates* while playing "Herod's Song" from the MCA album *Jesus Christ Superstar.* Start the film sequence at the point where the music's introductory ascending scale ends with a piano chord. Experiment a few times until you get the timing right.

ORDER OF WORSHIP

Prologue to Worship: Mark 15:37, 40:47

Call to Worship *(responsively)*
Christ is risen!
Christ is risen, indeed!
Let us celebrate the Resurrection as we worship God together!

Probe of the Word—Part One: The Transformation of the Place of Worship
Remove the black cloth from the cross. Have worshipers bring in decorations and put them in place while joyful music is played. When the transformation is complete, repeat the first two lines of the call to worship and have everyone applaud.

Hymn: "Jesus Christ Is Risen Today"

Affirmation of Faith *(unison)*
We believe in God, the creator of life and the giver of all good gifts.
We believe in Jesus the Christ, the one who defeated death and arose to new life.
We believe in the Holy Spirit, the spirit of truth that lives in us even today.
We believe in the church, the caring community that carries on the work of
    Jesus in the world.
We know that God loves us, and we are unafraid.
    We believe in new life—both in this world and in the world to come.
    We face the future without fear,
    Through Jesus Christ, our Lord. Amen.

The Gloria Patri

Scripture: Mark 16:1-7

Probe of the Word—Part Two: The Easter Excitement
Discuss the Scripture selections. Have participants brainstorm various words to express the feelings that they think were experienced by the women in the story—both before and after the Resurrection. Then have participants give words to express the feelings that they had both before and after the decoration of the room. Help them to become aware of the excitement and the exhilaration that Easter offers to everyone. Read expressions of hope from Worship Service No. 20.

Offering and Doxology

Prayer of Thanksgiving *(unison)*
O God, we thank you for the way that Easter has changed our lives. Because of Easter, we can never be the same again. Keep the Easter faith and the Easter feelings alive in us, through Jesus Christ our risen Lord. Amen.

Hymn: "Thine Is the Glory"

Benediction: Matthew 28:16-20 *(to be read by the worship leader)*

WORSHIP SERVICE NO. 34: "DANCE FOR JOY!"
(Following Easter)

Guidelines for the Basic Service

Purpose: To give worshipers an opportunity to participate in a worship service in which they express the Easter joy through the medium of dance.

Resources and Materials Needed: Bibles; hymnals; record player or cassette player and records *or pre-recorded tapes of music (optional)*

Hymns. The two suggested hymns are found in many hymnals. Alternative ideas are given in "Additional Ideas for This Service."

Offering and Doxology. This section is optional. For ideas on Doxologies, see "Additional Hymns and Service Music" in Part Three of this book.

Scripture. Second Samuel 6:12-15 tells how David danced before God in order to express his joy over the rescue of the Covenant Box (the Ark of the Covenant) from the Philistines. Exodus 15:19-21 tells how Moses' sister Miriam led a group of women in joyful singing and dancing to celebrate God's victory over the Egyptians at the Red Sea. Psalms 150 is a hymn of praise that urges people to praise God with music and dancing. The TEV is preferred for all selections.

Probe of the Word. This part of the service is designed to give participants an opportunity to praise God through dancing. You should be sensitive to persons who might be reluctant to participate in this activity. Gentle persuasion is recommended; but if some individuals absolutely refuse to dance, don't push them. As an alternative, some persons can stand on the sidelines and clap their hands and sing.

The suggested dance is a slow circle dance that is easy to learn. For directions, see the instructions and the illustrations in the probe itself. If your group is particularly adept at dancing, you may want to use faster music and have the group do more intricate dance steps.

Afterward, discuss the dance and participants' feelings about it.

Additional Ideas for This Service

If you have additional time and/or resources, you may wish to consider some of the following suggestions for alteration of the basic service:

Hymns. Substitute standard hymns or folk hymns for those suggested in the basic service. (1) *Standard Hymns:* "Rejoice, Ye Pure in Heart"; "O Happy Day, That Fixed My Choice"; or any of the hymns in the Easter section of your hymnal. (2) *Folk Hymns:* "And the Father Will Dance"; "Dance in the Darkness" *(Abba, Father)*; "Lord of the Dance" *(Songbook for Saints and Sinners, The Genesis Songbook)*.

Recorded Music for Dancing. Use one of the following selections as an alternative musical accompaniment for the dancing activity in the probe: "Day by Day"; "Light of the World" (from the Bell Records album of *Godspell*); "And the Father Will Dance" (from Carey Landry's album *Abba, Father,* available at many Catholic bookstores or from North American Liturgy Resources, 2110 W. Peoria Avenue, Phoenix, Arizona 85029).

Movies. Use one of the following movies: (1) *The Dancing Prophet* (16mm, color, 15 minutes, produced by Franciscan Communications Center). A film about Doug Crutchfield, a man who expresses his Christian faith through dance. (2) *Worship and the Arts: Liturgical Dance* (16mm, color, 11 minutes, produced by Leonora Pirret Hudson). A film about the use of liturgical dance in worship.

For information on film rentals, see "Movies" in Part Three of this book.

ORDER OF WORSHIP

Call to Worship (*responsively*)
It is the season of Eastertide! It is time to rejoice!
We are happy to be here! We are filled with joy!
Then let us worship God as we sing and dance together.

Hymn: "Come, Christians, Join to Sing"

Prayer of Reflection (*unison*)
O God, we praise you for the promise of new life that comes to us in this season. We thank you for Jesus' victory over death. We thank you for the vision of hope and happiness that his victory brings to our lives.

We want to praise you with our whole being. We want to dance and sing and celebrate. We want to express our joy by jumping up and down and shouting and clapping our hands.

Send your Spirit into our lives, so that we may move to the music and feel your joy flooding in upon us. Amen.

Offering and Doxology

Scripture: 2 Samuel 6:12-15; Exodus 15:19-21; Psalms 150

Probe of the Word: Praise God With Dancing
Have everyone assemble in a circle and join hands (as in Figure 1 or Figure 2). Then have everyone sing the following song (to the tune of "Jacob's Ladder") and do the circle dance as given in the instructions for the first stanza:

1. "Let us dance the dance of David! *(4 side steps to the left)*
   Let us dance the dance of David! *(4 side steps to the right)*
   Let us dance the dance of David! *(4 side steps to the left)*
   Dance before the Lord!" *(3 front steps while raising arms)*
2. "We will dance to Miriam's music!
   We will dance to Miriam's music!
   We will dance to Miriam's music!
   Dance before the Lord!"
3. "Dance with joy! Rejoice in Jesus!
   Dance with Joy! Rejoice in Jesus!
   Dance with joy! Rejoice in Jesus!
   Dance before the Lord!"

CIRCLE DANCE

Figure 1: Holding Hands With Adjacent Partners

Figure 2: Holding Hands With Alternate Partners

Figure 3: Side Step (left)   **Figure 4: Side Step (right)**   **Figure 5: Front Step**

Hymn: "All People That on Earth Do Dwell"

Benediction (*to be said by the worship leader*)
Go forth to praise God with your hearts, your minds, and your bodies! Amen.

WORSHIP SERVICE NO. 35: "WE ARE ONE"

Guidelines for the Basic Service

Purpose: To give persons an opportunity to worship God through a celebration of the unity of God's people.

Resources and Materials Needed: Bibles; hymnals; rope (¼" diameter) *or* small-link chain; knife (to cut rope) *or* chain-cutter (available on loan from some hardware stores)

Hymns. The two suggested hymns are found in many hymnals. Alternative ideas are given in "Additional Ideas for This Service."

Offering and Doxology. This section is optional. For ideas on Doxologies, see "Additional Hymns and Service Music" in Part Three of this book.

Scripture. All of the Biblical passages focus on the theme of unity—unity with God and with one another. The TEV is preferred for Psalms 133 and for the selections from John.

Probe of the Word. This part of the service should be done seriously—with emphasis on the connection between the acted-out parable of the rope or chain and the message of Ephesians 4:1-6.

Additional Ideas for This Service

If you have additional time and/or resources, you may wish to consider some of the following suggestions for alteration of the basic service:

Hymns. Substitute standard hymns or folk hymns for those suggested in the basic service. Folk hymn suggestions: "Tear Down the Walls" (in "Additional Hymns and Service Music" in Part Three of this book); "They'll Know We Are Christians by Our Love" (*Songbook for Saints and Sinners, The Genesis Songbook,* and other collections); "I'd Like to Teach the World to Sing" (*The Genesis Songbook*); and "I Believe in You" (*Close Your Eyes; I Got a Surprise*).

Other standard hymns that could be used in the service are: "In Christ There Is No East or West"; "Break Forth, O Living Light of God"; "One Holy Church of God Appears."

Movies. You may wish to use a movie on the theme of unity. Suggestions are: (1) *Baptism: Sacrament of Belonging* (16mm, color, 8 minutes, produced by Franciscan Communication Center). The story of how a community of Christian children accepts Alfredo, a homeless boy with a fire-scarred face. (2) *Nail* (16mm, color, 20 minutes, produced by Family Films). A modern parable that shows how a nail in a pot of soup water helps alienated apartment dwellers find fellowship and community.

For information on film rentals, see "Movies" in Part Three of this book.

ORDER OF WORSHIP

Call to Worship *(responsively)*

We have come here as individual persons. We come from different families and backgrounds. We have different abilities, talents, and interests.

We are thankful for the variety that enriches our lives.

As we gather as individuals, we discover our unity with one another. We are united by our Lord Jesus Christ, who makes all people one.

We are thankful for the unity that we experience as we follow our Lord.

Let us worship together and celebrate the unity and community that we find in our fellowship with our Lord and with one another.

Hymn: "Blest Be the Tie That Binds"

Prayer of Reflection *(unison)*

O God of Life, you have created us to be brothers and sisters together in your world. We are united with you and with one another. Yet we often emphasize our differences rather than our unity. We divide ourselves on the basis of race, nationality, gender, age, education, appearances, wealth. Turn our eyes from the differences that divide us. Focus our minds on the ways in which we are alike: our shared humanity, our need for you, our need for one another. Help us to see our various gifts to enrich one another's lives. Help us to worship as a unified people, through Jesus, our Brother and our Savior. Amen.

Scripture from the Old Testament: Psalms 133:1

Offering and Doxology

Scripture from the Gospel: John 13:34-35; 17:21-23

Probe of the Word: A Symbol of Unity

Have everyone gather in a circle and hold onto the rope or chain. Read Ephesians 4:1-6. Talk about some of the things that unify your group (*examples:* your belief in Jesus Christ; your fellowship experiences; service projects through which you have worked together to help someone in need.)

Point out the symbolism of the rope or chain: It links you together as a visible sign of your unity. Point out the importance of each section of the rope or chain: There can be no weak sections; everyone must be committed to the purposes and activities of your group. Then state that you are going to give each person a symbolic reminder of your group's unity. Cut the rope or chain into sections and give each person a piece to take with him or her.

Hymn: "Blest Be the Dear Uniting Love"

Benediction *(to be said by the worship leader)*

Go into the world to do God's work. Go as a member of this community of believers. Take Christian love and fellowship with you and offer them as gifts to everyone you meet. Amen.

WORSHIP SERVICE NO. 36: "FROM DEATH TO LIFE"

Guidelines for the Basic Service

Purpose: To give persons an opportunity to participate in a worship service in which they learn how to cope with death more effectively.

Resources and Materials Needed: Bibles; hymnals; pencils and paper; newsprint and markers, *or* chalkboard, chalk, and an eraser

Hymns. The two suggested hymns are found in many hymnals. Alternative ideas are given in "Additional Ideas for This Service."

Offering and Doxology. This section is optional. For ideas on Doxologies, see "Additional Hymns and Service Music" in Part Three of this book.

Scripture. First Corinthians 15 is Paul's great chapter on the Resurrection and life after death. In verses 12-22, there is a discussion of those who doubt life after death. In verses 35-38 and 42-44, Paul discusses the form that the resurrected body will take: it is to be a "spiritual body," which will have both physical and non-physical attributes. In verses 51-57, Paul talks about the final resurrection at the end of time. Verse 51 must be understood against the background of Paul's time, when it was thought that the end of the world would come soon. One of the alternate readings for this verse in an ancient New Testament manuscript says: "We shall all die"—with the "not" omitted. It is more probably that the original did include the "not." The TEV is preferred.

Probe of the Word. This part of the service is designed to be an in-depth discussion of death, grief, and life after death. You may wish to invite your pastor, a hospital chaplain, a hospice worker, and/or other persons who counsel the dying to serve as resource persons during the probe.

Additional Ideas for This Service

If you have additional time and/or resources, you may wish to consider some of the following suggestions for alteration of the basic service:

Hymns. Substitute standard hymns or folk hymns for those suggested in the basic service. (1) *Standard Hymns:* Substitute any of the hymns in the Easter section of your hymnal for the hymns in the basic service. (2) *Folk Hymns:* Alternatives for the *first* hymn: "Morning Has Broken" (*The Genesis Songbook*); "Allelu" (*Songbook for Saints and Sinners, The Genesis Songbook*); "I Was Glad" (*The Genesis Songbook, Avery and Marsh Songbook*); "Every Morning Is Easter Morning" (*Avery and Marsh Songbook*); "Alle, Alle" (*Songbook for Saints and Sinners*); "Jesus Is Life"; "In Him We Live" (both in *Abba, Father*); "You Are the Way" (*A New Commandment*).

Alternatives for the *second* hymn: "Lord of the Dance" (*Songbook for Saints and Sinners, The Genesis Songbook*); "Anything Happens" (*Wherever You Go*); "Peace" (*Locusts and Wild Honey*); "I Lift Up My Eyes" (*Songbook for Saints and Sinners*).

Movie. Use the movie *Though I Walk Through the Valley* (16mm, color, 30 minutes, produced by Pyramid Films), which is a documentary about the death of a man named Tony Brouwer. A message about resurrection is presented by the use of early sequences in reverse order after the scene of Brouwer's funeral.

For information on film rentals, see "Movies" in Part Three of this book.

ORDER OF WORSHIP

Call to Worship *(responsively)*
God is eternal! In God *we* have the hope of eternal life!
We want to have that life-giving hope! We want to discover life that can conquer even death itself!
Then let us worship the eternal God, so that we may find the victory of life.

Hymn: "The Day of Resurrection"

Prayer of Reflection *(unison)*
O God, we know that you are the source of all life. We know that you sent your Son Jesus to give us life in all its fullness.

We want to sing out hallelujahs of hope and life. We want to be able to believe that you will be with us even beyond death.

But it is difficult for us to deal with death. We are crushed by pain when we have to part with those we love. We face our own deaths with fear and confusion.

O God, heal our unbelief. Send your Spirit to inspire us with faith and hope, so that we may face the future without fear and be certain that we will live on in a new life that never ends, through Jesus Christ our Lord. Amen.

Offering and Doxology

Scripture: 1 Corinthians 15: 12-22, 35-38, 42-44, 51-57

Probe of the Word: Dealing With Death
Give each person a pencil and a piece of paper. Divide the group into teams of two or three persons. Have the teams discuss and write out responses to the following questions:

1. What relatives or close friends of yours have died? What feelings did you have about those deaths? Have you "worked through" those feelings? If so, how?

2. How do you feel about your own death? Are you afraid of death? Why or why not?

3. Have you heard or read stories of people who have been "brought back to life" after "near-death" experiences? If so, what reports did these people give about their experiences? How do you feel about these reports?

4. Do you believe the Biblical accounts of Jesus' Resurrection? Why or why not? Do you believe that you will live on after death? Why or why not? If you believe in life after death, what do you think the after-life will be like?

5. How can your Christian faith help you in dealing with death?

Afterward, collate and discuss responses. Give particular attention to how the scriptural selections relate to the responses.

Conclude with a prayer in which you ask God to give you faith in God's promise of eternal life through Jesus Christ.

Hymn: "I Know That My Redeemer Lives"

Benediction *(to be said by the worship leader)*
Go forth in joy! Go forth with faith and hope! Live your life in the knowledge that God gives new life that continues even beyond death! Amen.

WORSHIP SERVICE NO. 37: "CELEBRATE LIFE!"

Guidelines for the Basic Service

Purpose: To give persons an opportunity to celebrate the joys of their lives in a worship service.

Resources and Materials Needed: Bibles; hymnals; pencils and pieces of paper; offering plate(s) (optional)

Hymns. The two suggested hymns are found in many hymnals. Alternative ideas are given in "Additional Ideas for This Service."

Offering and Doxology. This section is optional, but it is recommended that it be included. For ideas on Doxologies, see "Additional Hymns and Service Music" in Part Three of this book.

Scripture. Deuteronomy is part of Moses' speech to the people of Israel as they prepare to enter the Promised Land. Moses urges them to be the true people of God by choosing God's way of life and following God's commandments. In John 10:7-10, Jesus states that he is the gate for the sheep and that he has come in order to bring life in all its fullness. The TEV is preferred for both selections.

Probe of the Word. This part of the service is designed to give participants an opportunity to celebrate some of the joys of their lives.

Additional Ideas for This Service

If you have additional time and/or resources, you may wish to consider some of the following suggestions for alteration of the basic service:

Hymns. Substitute standard hymns or folk hymns for those suggested in the basic service. (1) *Standard Hymns:* Substitute one of the following hymns for either of the hymns suggested in the basic service: "O Happy Day, That Fixed My Choice"; "O How Happy Are They"; "We, Thy People, Praise Thee."

(2) *Folk Hymns:* Substitute one of the following hymns for either of the hymns suggested in the basic service: "You Can Tell the World" (*Exodus Songbook*); "We're Here to Be Happy" (*The Genesis Songbook*); "Happiness" (*Wherever You Go*); "Joy That Knows No End" (*Locusts and Wild Honey*); "I Was Glad" (*Exodus Songbook, Avery and Marsh Songbook*); "Every Morning Is Easter Morning" (*Avery and Marsh Songbook*); "Joy Is Like the Rain" (*Joy Is Like the Rain*); "Thanks Be to God" (*Songbook for Saints and Sinners*)—may also be sung to the tune of the old song "Windy" by the group, The Association; "Come On and Celebrate!"; "Sing This Song and Celebrate" (both in "Additional Hymns and Service Music" in Part Three of this book).

Recorded Music. Use recorded music for a prelude, offertory, and/or postlude. Suggestions: "I Want to Live" from John Denver's RCA album *I Want to Live*; "Love Is Everywhere" from John Denver's RCA album *Windsong*; "I'm Alive" from Neil Diamond's Columbia album *Heartlight*. To create an audio-visual presentation, show slides of life-affirming happy scenes while the music is playing. For information on slide-and-music presentations, see pages 116-126 of the C-4 Resources book *Youth Workers' Handbook* or some of the media resources listed in Part Three of this book.

Movie. Use the movie *The String* (16mm, color, 18 minutes, produced by Film-Canada), which shows how a young woman uses a string to unite various people in a joyous celebration of their kinship.

For information on film rentals, see "Movies" in Part Three of this book.

ORDER OF WORSHIP

Call to Worship *(responsively)*
It is the season of Eastertide! It is the season of life and joy!
We are happy to be alive! We want to have the joy of Easter in our lives!
Then let us celebrate this season as we worship God together.

Hymn: "We, Thy People, Praise Thee"

Prayer of Reflection *(unison)*
O God, you are the giver of all good gifts. You give us the golden seasons of our lives. You fill our hearts with joy.
Forgive us for taking your gifts for granted. Forgive us for our failure to celebrate the fullness of our lives.
Help us discover the joys that surround us. Show us how to celebrate and be happy, through Christ our Lord. Amen.

Scripture: Deuteronomy 30:15-20; John 10:7-10

Probe of the Word: Celebrating the Joys of Life
Give each worshiper a pencil and a piece of paper. Have persons work individually to write out at least one response in each of the following categories:

1. I am joyful about myself because _____.

2. People in my family give me joy by _____.

3. My friends give me joy by _____.

4. I find joy in being a Christian because _____.

5. When I look at the world around me, I rejoice because of _____

_____.

After everyone has finished, divide the group into teams of two or three persons. Have team members share voluntarily with one another.
Then reassemble as a full group. Have team members share with the full group by reporting the responses of other persons in their teams. (*Note:* Again, the sharing should be voluntary. No person should share another person's response if the person making that response does not want it to be shared.)
After the group sharing period, have participants fold their sheets and place them—along with any offerings of money—in the offering plate(s) or on the altar during the offering.

Offering and Doxology

Prayer of Dedication *(unison)*
O God, we thank you for the joys of our lives. We praise you as we present our celebrations of life. Help us always to remember the many joyful blessings that you have given us. Show us how to be thankful. Show us how to live our lives with the joy of Jesus in our hearts. Amen.

Hymn: "Rejoice, the Lord Is King"

Benediction *(to be said by the worship leader)*
Go forth to live happy and joyful lives, through Christ our Lord! Amen.

WORSHIP SERVICE NO. 38: "GOD'S NATURAL WORLD"

Guidelines for the Basic Service

Purpose: To give persons an opportunity to participate in a worship service in which they become more aware of their responsibility to care for the natural world.

Resources and Materials Needed: Bibles; hymnals; pencils and paper; newsprint and markers, *or* chalkboard, chalk, and eraser; pictures of nature scenes; potted plants and flowers; natural items such as pine cones, sea shells, stones; offering plate(s) (optional)

Hymns. The two suggested hymns are found in many hymnals. Alternative ideas are given in "Additional Ideas for This Service."

Offering and Doxology. This section is optional, but it is recommended that it be included. For ideas on Doxologies, see "Additional Hymns and Service Music" in Part Three of this book.

Scripture. Psalms 19 proclaims that God's glory is revealed in the natural world every day. Psalms 24:1-2 is a reminder that everything in the world belongs to God. In Genesis 1:26-31, God creates human beings and gives them responsibility for taking care of the natural world. The TEV is preferred for all the selections.

Probe of the Word. This part of the service is designed to help participants become more aware of the beauty of the natural world and to help them learn how to be better stewards of the world.

In order to create a good environment for the service and the probe, you should decorate the worship place with nature items such as those listed in the resources and materials section above.

Additional Ideas for This Service

If you have additional time and/or resources, you may wish to consider some of the following suggestions for alteration of the basic service:

Hymns. Substitute any of the following standard hymns or folk hymns for either of the hymns suggested in the basic service: (1) *Standard Hymns:* "God of the Earth, the Sky, the Sea"; "All Beautiful the March of Days"; "Let All on Earth Their Voices Raise"; "The Spacious Firmament on High"; "This Is My Father's World."

(2) *Folk Hymns:* "Morning Has Broken" (*The Genesis Songbook*); "This Is My Father's World"; "Psalm of Thanksgiving" (both in *Exodus Songbook*); "Anything Happens" (*Wherever You Go*); "Joy That Knows No End" (*Locusts and Wild Honey*); "Joy Is Like the Rain" (*Joy Is Like the Rain*).

Solo. Have a soloist sing "What Have They Done to the Rain?" (*The Genesis Songbook*).

Recorded Music. Use recorded music for a prelude, offertory, and/or postlude. Suggestions: The following songs by John Denver—"Sunshine on My Shoulders" from his RCA album *John Denver's Greatest Hits*; "Eclipse" from his RCA album *Back Home Again*; "Calypso" or "Windsong" from his RCA album *Windsong*. To create an audio-visual presentation, show nature slides with any of these songs.

Movie. Use the movie *The Eighth Day* (16mm, color, 12 minutes, produced by A. Scott Miller), which presents a panorama of the natural world accompanied by narration from the Psalms.

For information on film rentals, see "Movies" in Part Three of this book.

ORDER OF WORSHIP

Call to Worship *(responsively)*
God created the world!
God proclaims that the world is good!
Let us praise the God of all creation as we worship together!

Hymn: "For the Beauty of the Earth"

Prayer of Reflection *(unison)*
O God, we are amazed at the wonders of your world. We stand in awe of your works—the glory of the galaxies, the miracle of the microbes, the marvel of human life. Even with our newest knowledge and our state-of-the-art computers, we cannot comprehend your creation, we cannot calculate its infinite complexities.

O God, we do not begin to understand the secrets of the universe, but we are blessed by its beauty. We have not discovered the deepest truths about the world of nature, but we know that it proclaims your presence.

Gives us a sense of reverence for the created world. Deliver us from those actions that destroy the beauty and balance of nature. Teach us how to be concerned caretakers, so we may preserve the precious gift of our splendid environment. Amen.

Scripture: Psalms 19; Psalms 24:1-2; Genesis 1:26-31

Probe of the Word: Caring for God's Natural World
Give each participant a pencil and a piece of paper. Have persons work individually to write on the first sheet some actions that are harmful to the natural world and on the second sheet some actions that people can take to help preserve the beauty and balance of the natural world.

After everyone has finished, collate responses in two columns on newsprint or a chalkboard. Give particular attention to the suggestions for improving the quality of the natural world. Have participants choose some suggestions for group action and some for individual action. Make action plans.

In preparation for the offering, have participants fold the sheets containing their suggestions for positive actions and place them—along with any gifts of money—in the offering plate(s) or on the altar during the offering.

Offering and Doxology

Prayer of Dedication *(unison)*
O God, we offer ourselves, our gifts, and our ideas to you. Use us, our gifts, and our abilities for your purposes. Make us better stewards of your gift of the natural world, through Jesus Christ our Lord. Amen.

Hymn: "All Things Bright and Beautiful"

Benediction *(to be said by the worship leader)*
The Bible tells us that God created the world in seven days! It is now "the eighth day of creation"—that ever-continuing day when we are to work creatively to preserve the natural world! Go forth to care for the world and the environment! Amen.

WORSHIP SERVICE NO. 39: "THE CHURCH IS BORN!"
(Day of Pentecost)

Guidelines for the Basic Service

Purpose: To give persons an opportunity to participate in a worship service in which they gain a deeper understanding of the birth of the church on Pentecost Day.

Resources and Materials Needed: Bibles; hymnals; pencils and index cards; a birthday cake; cookies; juice; balloons and other party items (optional)

Hymns. The two suggested hymns are found in many hymnals. Alternative ideas are given in "Additional Ideas for This Service."

Offering and Doxology. This section is optional. For ideas on Doxologies, see "Additional Hymns and Service Music" in Part Three of this book.

Scripture. Genesis 11:1-9 tells the familiar story of the Tower of Babel (or Babylon). The story points out the problems caused by lack of community and communication. You should spend some time coaching the reader in the pronunciation of the place names in the narrative, or you may choose to omit the verse containing these names. Acts 2:1-11 tells of the Day of Pentecost, when the Holy Spirit was given to Jesus' followers and the church was born. This story emphasizes the value of true community and good communication. The TEV is recommended for both selections.

Probe of the Word. This part of the service gives the group an opportunity to have a party as they approach the end of the school year. The party is a birthday party for the church—similar to the birthday party for Jesus in the Christmas Sunday service. You may wish to add an extra touch by having the words "Happy Birthday to the Church" on the cake and using birthday candles (perhaps twenty candles—one for each century of the church's existence). Other ideas: balloons, posters, noisemakers, and other party items.

Prior to the party, there will be a simulation game designed to give participants a sense of the lack of communication at Babel (or Babylon) and the restoration of communication on the day of Pentecost. Prepare for this activity in advance by making several sets of "language cards." There should be two or three cards to a set, and the words on the cards in each set should be identical nonsense words. You may choose to make up words of your own or to use some of the following suggestions: ah-GAH-too; dip-ee-NOO-lah; no-no-yo-BAH; zip-zip-CLACK; dum-dum-dee-DAH; mee-YAH-nah; nah-nah-BAH-nah; wah-hoo-YAH-hoo; ah-bah-LEE-bah; kee-lah-sah-DUM.

Additional Ideas for This Service

If you have additional time and/or resources, you may wish to consider some of the following suggestions for alteration of the basic service:

Hymns. Substitute any of the following standard hymns or folk hymns for either of the hymns suggested in the basic service: (1) *Standard Hymns:* "Christ Is Made the Sure Foundation"; "One Holy Church of God Appears"; "Holy Spirit, Truth Divine"; "Come, Holy Ghost, Our Hearts Inspire"; (2) *Folk Hymns:* "Canticle for Pentecost" (*The Genesis Songbook*); "The Church Within Us" (*The Genesis Songbook, Songbook for Saints and Sinners*); "If There is a Holy Spirit"; "We Are the Church" (both in *Avery and Marsh Songbook*); "Everyone Moved by the Spirit" (*Abba, Father*).

Movie. Use the movie *One Who Was There* (16mm, color, 37 minutes, produced by United Methodist Communications), which tells of one of Jesus' friends, a woman who finds her faith renewed thirty years after his death by an encounter with some joyful Christians. Rental information is given in "Movies" in Part Three of this book.

ORDER OF WORSHIP

Call to Worship *(responsively)*
Today is the Day of Pentecost!
Today is the birthday of the Church!
Let us celebrate this day and this season, so that the church may be reborn in us.

Hymn: "The Church's One Foundation"

Prayer of Reflection *(unison)*
O God of our past, present, and future:
We thank you for the church;
We thank you for caring communities within congregations;
We thank you for the hopeful word that the church speaks to a hurting world.
On this Day of Pentecost,
Send the wind of your Spirit to shake us loose from our old ways;
Send the fire of your spirit to burn away the barren places in our lives;
Send the force of your Spirit to fill us with faith and power. Amen.

Offering and Doxology

Scripture: Genesis 11:1-9; Acts 2:1-11

Probe of the Word: A Pentecost Celebration
Hand out the "language cards" at random. Tell participants that each person is to wander around the room and continuously shout out his or her nonsense word until he or she finds another person (or other persons) chanting the same word. Then persons with the same word are to sit down together and talk about good aspects of the church. (Don't be bothered if some persons consider this activity somewhat silly and foolish. You may wish to agree that it is somewhat silly and then to point out that the foolishness of it all can be a source of fun and humor and that participants will probably enjoy the experience once they get into it.)

Afterward, discuss the activity. Give particular attention to how this experience relates to the two Scripture selections.

After the discussion, light the candles on the cake and sing "Happy Birthday" to the church (or "Happy Birthday" from *Avery and Marsh Songbook*). Then lead the group in applause (and noise-making if you have noise-makers available) and blow out the candles. Conclude the celebration by serving the cake, cookies, and juice.

After the party, talk about the meaning of the Day of Pentecost. Emphasize the way in which the coming of the Holy Spirit enabled people to communicate with one another and become a true community. Then offer a prayer in which you ask God to give the gift of the Spirit to your group.

Hymn: "Spirit of Life, In This New Dawn"

Benediction *(to be said by the worship leader)*
Go forth to be Spirit-filled people! Take the love of this community with you and communicate it to a world that is torn and divided! Amen.

WORSHIP SERVICE NO. 40: "SAYING GOODBYE"

Guidelines for the Basic Service

Purpose: To help members of a group find in worship a means of affirming their unity as they prepare to separate.

Resources and Materials Needed: Bibles; hymnals; poster of Numbers 6:24-26

Hymns. The two suggested hymns are found in many hymnals. If you use the hymn "O God, Our Help in Ages Past," omit the stanza beginning "A thousand ages . . ." and the stanza beginning "Time, like an ever rolling stream. . . ." For alternative ideas on hymns, see "Additional Ideas for This Service."

Offering and Doxology. This section is optional. For ideas on Doxologies, see "Additional Hymns and Service Music" in Part Three of this book.

Scripture. Psalms 121 affirms that God watches over us at all times and protects us as we come and go. Numbers 6:24-26 is the famous Old Testament benediction used by many youth groups. The passage from John gives part of Jesus' farewell to his disciples—words promising God's gift of peace and the spirit.

Probe of the Word. Prepare for this activity by posting the words of Numbers 6:24-26 in the room.

Additional Ideas for This Service

If you have additional time and/or resources, you may wish to consider some of the following suggestions for alteration of the basic service:

Hymns. Substitute standard hymns or folk hymns for those suggested in the basic service. Alternatives for the *first* hymn: (1) *Standard Hymns:* "For the Beauty of the Earth"; "We, Thy People, Praise Thee"; (2) *Folk Hymns:* "Day by Day" (*Genesis Songbook*); "They'll Know We Are Christians by Our Love" (*Songbook for Saints and Sinners, Genesis Songbook,* and other collections).

Alternatives for the *second* hymn: (1) *Standard Hymns:* "Blest Be the Dear Uniting Love"; "God Be With You Till We Meet Again"; (2) *Folk Hymns:* "Goodbye" (*Avery and Marsh Songbook*); "Shalom Chaverim" (*Songbook for Saints and Sinners, Exodus Songbook,* and other collections); "You've Got a Friend" (*Exodus Songbook*); "Peace" (*Locusts and Wild Honey*).

A Musical Benediction. Have the group or a soloist sing "Benediction" (in "Additional Hymns and Service Music" in Part Three of this book) after—or instead of—the benediction in the basic service.

Recorded Music. Use one of these recordings as a prelude and the other as a postlude: "Friends With You" (from John Denver's RCA album *Aerie*); "Wherever You Go" (from the album of the same name by the Monks of Weston Priory). For information on the Weston Priory album, see "Recordings" in Part Three of this book.

You may wish to use these songs as hymns. The Denver song is in the songbook *Aerie* (Cherry Lane Music Co., 1971); the Weston Priory song is in the songbook *Wherever You Go*.

The words from the spoken part of "Wherever You Go" would make an excellent poster for use in this service. Transcribe the words from the book or the record.

ORDER OF WORSHIP

Call to Worship *(responsively)*
We gather together as the people of God.
We are a community of friends who love God and one another.
We gather together to prepare ourselves for separation.
We ask God to guide us on our separate journeys.
Let us worship our God—the one who blesses our gathering and our going forth.

Hymn: "O God, Our Help in Ages Past"

Prayer of Reflection *(unison)*
Lord of life, we stand at one of life's crossroads. We are preparing to say goodbye. Give us the courage to be open to our mixed emotions, to affirm freely both our joy in our fellowship and our sadness in saying farewell.

Enable us to celebrate the positive ways in which our lives have touched one another—the love and laughter, the care and concern, the warm embraces and happy words. Enable us also to affirm our struggles together—the anger, the anguish, the grief, and the disagreements. Help us to realize the growth and the grace that have come not only from moments of mutual support but also from our differences and disagreements.

O God, go with us in the sorrow of separation. Lighten our burden by reminding us that the times we have known together will always be a source of support and strength. As we leave this place, may your love and your spirit keep us united with one another and with you, through Jesus Christ our Lord. Amen.

Scripture: Psalms 121

Offering and Doxology.

Probe of the Word: "Saying Goodbye"
Have everyone (including the worship leader) stand in a circle and join hands. Go around the circle two times and ask for responses. The first time, have each person say aloud the following incomplete sentence and complete it in his or her own words: *Being in this group has been meaningful to me because. . . .* The second time, use this incomplete sentence: *As we say goodbye, my wish for the members of this group—or for   (name)   , who is leaving this group—is. . . .*

Then have everyone pray together the words of Numbers 6:24-26. Afterward, say: *When Jesus was preparing to leave his disciples for the last time, he told them that they would always be united by their love for him, for God, and for one another. He reminded them that the spirit would support and strengthen them and that they would receive the gift of peace—God's "shalom," which means "wholeness," "integrity," and "well-being."* Close by reading John 14:16-18, 27-31.

Hymn: "Blest Be the Tie That Binds"

Benediction *(to be said by the worship leader)*
We have experienced what it means to be united in a covenant with God and with one another. This covenant will never be broken. As we go forth from this place, may this covenant always keep us together in a spirit of love and unity. Amen.

SERVICES FOR CAMP OR RETREAT SETTINGS

INTRODUCTION

The two services in this section are designed for occasions when your group is involved in a camp or a retreat. The first service relates to the theme of self-discovery. The second service is a celebration of joy in the out-of-doors.

Here are some introductory notes on the services:

Finding My Self. This service gives worshipers an opportunity to get in touch with their own feelings and gain some insights about their relationships with God. The service includes some recorded music. If you do not have the suggested recordings and either a record player or a cassette player, you will need to alter the service by substituting other service components.

You should feel free to substitute any of your group's favorite "camp hymns" (such as those found in *Lift Every Voice* and other camp songbooks) for the hymns suggested in the service.

Enjoy! Enjoy! This service gives worshipers an opportunity to celebrate their good feelings about fun in the out-of-doors. The service is designed so that it may be done in an outdoor setting. No media items or electricity will be necessary. Here again, you should feel free to substitute your group's favorite "camp hymns" (such as those found in *Lift Every Voice* and other camp songbooks) for the hymns suggested in the service.

Note: Although these services are specifically designed for camp or retreat settings, they may also be used for other settings. Likewise, many of the forty services in the preceding section of this book may be used for camps or retreats—in most cases with little or no alteration necessary.

WORSHIP SERVICE NO. 1: "FINDING MY SELF"

The Prelude: Recorded Music—"The Wind" —Cat Stevens

The Call to Worship *(responsively)*
God is calling to us! God wants us to listen!
We want to hear God's voice!
Let us worship God together, so that we may hear God's word.
Let us seek God's presence, so that we may discover ourselves.

The Hymn of Praise: "Canticle for Pentecost"

The Readings from the Old Testament: 1 Kings 19:1-13; Deuteronomy 30:11-15 *(TEV)*

The Prayer of Reflection *(unison)*
O God, like Elijah, we have tried to find the meaning of life in the big events of our time. We have sought security in the wisdom of the world, but it has been like a wayward wind—showering dust and debris upon our despair. We have looked for a message in machines and technology, but they have been like an earthquake—causing us to be shaken and confused. We have looked for happiness in the latest fads and fashions, but they have burned out like a dying fire—leaving ashes and emptiness behind.

O God, speak to us as you spoke to Elijah and Moses. When our lives are like a vacuum, whisper to us in a soft voice. When we roam about and look far and wide for your word, center us down on your presence within our selves.

Help us to pause and ponder. Speak to us through the Spirit that is in each of us. Show us how to meditate in our minds and hearts, so that we may find the meaning of our lives. Amen.

The Offering
Offertory: Recorded Music—"Looking for Space" —John Denver

The Doxology

The Hymn of Meditation: "Kum Ba Yah"

The Silent Meditation

The Lord's Prayer *(unison)*

The Hymn of Preparation: "Breathe on Me, Breath of God"

The Readings from the New Testament: Luke 17:20-21; Luke 27:39-41 *(TEV)*

The Probe of the Word: Finding My Self
Discuss the New Testament Scriptures. Give special attention to Jesus' statement about finding the Kingdom of God "within you" and the fact that Jesus himself frequently went aside to a quiet place to meditate and pray.

Then have all participants go and find a quiet place for individual personal meditation and prayer. You may leave it to each person to decide how he or she will meditate, or you may choose to suggest meditation topics such as the following:

1. Some Things That I Want to Thank God For
2. Sins and Failures That I Would Like to Confess
3. Ways in Which I Want God to Help Me Change Myself
4. Aspects of My Life for Which I Want to Ask God's Guidance
5. Concerns I Have About Other Individuals

Allow about a half hour or so for meditation. Then call everyone back to the worship area (you may want to use a bell or some other signal that can be heard by everyone). Have voluntary sharing of thoughts and feelings about the experience. Then have everyone join in the following prayer.

The Prayer of Dedication *(unison)*

O God, we celebrate ourselves. We know that you have created us in your image and that you have sent your Spirit to dwell in us. Help us to center down on our inner selves, so that we may hear your voice and behold the vision of what we may become, through Christ our Lord. Amen.

The Hymn of Dedication: "Just a Closer Walk With Thee"

The Benediction *(to be said by the worship leader)*

Go forth into the world! Go forth to find God in the world around you! Go forth to find God in the wider world that is within you! Amen.

The Postlude: Recorded Music—"There's a World"

—Neil Young

* * * * * * * * * *

Notes

• **Hymns.** The hymn "Breathe on Me, Breath of God" is found in many hymnals; it is also found in some "camp songbooks." "Canticle for Pentecost," "Kum Ba Yah," and "Just a Closer Walk With Thee" are in *The Genesis Songbook.* "Kum Ba Yah" is also in *Songbook for Saints and Sinners* and some "camp songbooks."

• **Recorded Music.** "The Wind" is on Cat Stevens' A&M album *Teaser and the Firecat.* "Looking for Space" in on John Denver's RCA album *Windsong.* "There's a World" is on Neil Young's Reprise album *Harvest.*

• **Scripture.** The recommended version for all of the Scripture readings is *Today's English Version.*

WORSHIP SERVICE NO. 2: "ENJOY! ENJOY!"

The Call to Worship *(responsively)*
God sent Jesus into the world to give us a full and joyful life!
We want to have the happiness that Jesus offers to us!
Then let us worship God, so that our joy may be full and overflowing!

The Hymn of Praise: "We're Here to Be Happy"

The Prayer of Reflection *(unison)*
O God, the world is alive with the wonder of your presence.
We praise you for the beauty of your creation. We marvel at the majesty of the mountains, the quiet stillness of the lakes, the thundering sound of the roaring seas, the splashes of colors that flare up in the flowers.
When we look at ourselves, we become even more aware of your wonderful creative powers. You have made us in your own image. You have given us the breath of life. You have put hope and joy in our hearts.
O God, we thank you for the beauty of our bodies and the miracle of our minds. We thank you for the blessings that we enjoy—good food, loving families, caring friends, sports and games and other fun-filled activities.
Help us always to be aware of how fortunate we are. Fill our lives with fun and excitement, and fill our hearts with thankfulness. Amen.

The Offering

The Hymn of Thankfulness: "I Was Glad"

The Call to Meditation and Prayer *(responsively)*
May the joy of our Lord be with you!
May the joy of our Lord be with you, also!
Let us meditate in silence. Let us consider our many blessings, so that we may prepare ourselves to pray the prayer that Jesus taught us.

The Silent Meditation

The Lord's Prayer *(unison)*

The Hymn of Joy: "You Can Tell the World"

The Reading from the Scripture: John 10:7-10; John 15:9-11 *(TEV)*

The Probe of the Word: Celebrating Our Joy
Discuss the Scripture passages. Give special attention to the ways in which Jesus makes it possible for us to have full and joyful lives.
Divide the group into teams of two or three persons. Give each team a pencil and a sheet of paper. Have the teams brainstorm for a few minutes and list enjoyable things and activities—especially those related to the out-of-doors.
Afterward, assemble the whole group and have reporters from the teams share team members' responses with the group. After each team has reported, have everyone join in praying the following litany: *O God, we thank you for the joys that these persons have shared with us. Amen.*

The Hymn for Going Forth: "Go and Be Happy"

The Words of Joyful Praise *(to be said by the worship leader)*
Jude 24-25 *(Today's English Version)*

The Hymn of Benediction: "Shalom Chaverim"

* * * * * * * * *

Notes

Hymns. All of the hymns may be found in *The Genesis Songbook*. "Shalom Chaverim" may also be found in some "camp songbooks."

In some editions of *The Genesis Songbook*, there are three blank spaces in the lyrics for the last stanza of "I Was Glad." The word "am" should be inserted in each of these three spaces.

Resources and Materials Needed. You should have available pencils and paper for the team activity in the Probe of the Word.

YOUTH-LED CONGREGATIONAL WORSHIP SERVICES

INTRODUCTION

The three services in this section are designed for occasions when your youth group has the opportunity to lead the congregation in worship. Our main criterion for deciding which services to include in this section was the question of which occasions are usually open for youth-led services—a particularly crucial question in those churches that do not have a history of youth involvement in preparing and leading worship services.

With this criterion in mind, we have decided to include some services that would probably be acceptable to officials in most churches, even those that have never had a youth-led service. Our reasoning went something like this: (1) Most Good Friday services are held in the afternoon; and Good Friday evening is usually open for a new and different kind of service; (2) Many churches are willing to let young people do the sunrise service on Easter morning; indeed, in view of the early hour, many churches are *eager* for the youth to lead this service! (3) In almost all churches, the church officials are open to having the youth lead *at least one special youth service each year*—on student recognition day or a similar occasion.

Since these three services are all for special occasions, they are designed as complete entities in themselves. Unlike the weekly youth group services, they do not include a lot of suggestions for alteration of the services. It is assumed, however, that many groups will alter the services somewhat to make them more suitable for individual churches and situations.

Here are some introductory notes on the services:

"The Crucifixion: Then and Now" (Good Friday Evening Service). This is a multi-media service. Our rationale for designing the service this way: If you want to get people to come out for a service at a different time than usual, you should do something particularly new, exciting, and different!

A rehearsal is an *absolute must* for this service! You will probably want to have a service director, a supervisor of media, a drama coach, a music supervisor, and a liturgy supervisor. Make sure that all necessary media items are secured well in advance. Make copies of the order of worship.

Do a last-minute check of media equipment, staging for the play, and so forth just prior to the service.

"Morning Has Broken" (Easter Sunrise Service). This service is designed to be done outdoors. The music may be accompanied by guitars, flutes, and other portable instruments. To facilitate congregational singing, all the songs for this service may be found in *The Genesis Songbook*. You should make copies of the service for all worshipers. For "The Interpretation of the Word," have "mini-sermons" (about five minutes each) on the Easter hope or have persons read the "hope responses" from Worship Service No. 20: "Hope of the World" in the preceding section of this book.

From Generation to Generation" (Standard Sunday Service). This service is designed for a Sunday worship service in the church sanctuary. You will need to make copies of the service for all worshipers—probably on a standard church bulletin form. If the suggested hymns are not in your hymnal, you will need to make alternative selections. "The Interpretation of the Word" is to consist of three "mini-sermons" (about five minutes each) prepared and delivered by three young persons.

WORSHIP SERVICE NO. 1: "THE CRUCIFIXION: THEN AND NOW"
(A Multi-Media Worship Experience for Good Friday Evening)

The Prelude: "Some Folks' Lives Roll Easy" —Paul Simon
>(Recorded Music With Modern Dance Interpretation)

The Hymn of Self-Evaluation: "Were You There?" —American Folk Hymn

The Reading from the Gospel: Matthew 26:36-46 *(Today's English Version)*

Slide-and-Music Presentation: "Gethsemane" —From *Jesus Christ Superstar*
>*(Slides Showing Examples of Oppression in Modern Society)*

The Trial of Jesus: An Excerpt From *Christ in the Concrete City* —P.W. Turner

Scenes From Then and Now
>(Music: "Silent Night/Seven O'Clock News"—Paul Simon and Art Garfunkel)
>(Visuals: Scenes From the Life of Jesus; Scenes of Violence in Today's World)

The Crucifixion
>(Narration: Reading of Mark 15:16-39 in *Today's English Version)*
>(Music: "The Carriage of the Cross" From *The Robe)*
>(Visual: A Slide of Jesus on the Cross Projected Onto a Real Cross)

The Prayer of Confession *(unison)*
   O God, sensitize our sights so that we may see things as they really are. Enlarge our vision so that we may view the world as it ought to be.
   We confess before you that we often see only what we want to see.
   We seek luxurious life-styles and more money while thousands of poor people are dying from hunger and disease.
   We talk about equality and justice, but we judge people on the basis of the place of their birth, the color of their skin, the cost of their houses, their age and gender.
   We speak of peace, but we worship the weapons of war.
   We do not reach out as we should to help the poor, the sick, the prisoners, the lonely.
   O God, show us your way and your truth, so that we will not lie to ourselves.
   Have mercy upon us, and remind us that what we do to the least of these our brothers and sisters we do also to you.
   Forgive us, O God, and grant us new life, through Jesus Christ our Lord. Amen.

The Words of Forgiveness and Assurance *(to be said by the worship leader)*
   Jesus tells us: You are forgiven! Go in peace! Turn away from sin!
   I say to you: Whatever you have done in the past is truly in the past! You are accepted as you are in this present moment! The future is open to you! Walk and live in the light of God's love! Amen!

The Hymn of Assurance: "What Wondrous Love Is This?"

The Litany of Silence: A Period of Individual Meditation and Silent Prayer

The Postlude: "The Sound of Silence" —Paul Simon and Art Garfunkel
>(Recorded Music With Modern Dance Interpretation)

The Going Forth *(responsively)*
   We have met for this service of worship.
   We have been reminded of the Crucifixion of Jesus our Lord.
   We have been reminded of the ways in which persons crucify one another even today.
   We have prayed for forgiveness.
   We have the assurance of forgiveness and new life.
   The service is ended. Go in peace. Amen.

The Music for Going Forth: "Fantasia on a Theme of Thomas Tallis"
(Recorded Music: Composed by Ralph Vaughan Williams)

* * * * * * * * * *

Notes

• The song "Some Folks' Lives Roll Easy" is from Paul Simon's Columbia album *Still Crazy After All These Years*.

• *Hymns*. The two suggested hymns are found in many hymnals. Other Lenten hymns may be substituted.

• The Song "Gethsemane" is from the MCA album *Jesus Christ Superstar*.

• *Slides*. For information on making home-made slides and general information on slide-and-music presentations, see pages 116-126 of *Youth Workers' Handbook*, by Steve Clapp and Jerry O. Cook (C-4 Resources, 1983). Also see resources in the "Media" section in Part Three of this book.

• The excerpt from *Christ in the Concrete City*, by P.W. Turner (London: SPCK, 1967) is the section of the play found on pages 10-17. The language of this British play should be adapted for American audiences.

• The song "Silent Night/Seven O'Clock News" is from Simon and Garfunkel's Columbia album *Parsley, Sage, Rosmary, and Thyme*.

• *Movies*. As an alternative to slides in "Scenes From Then and Now," you may wish to use these two movies: *The Face of Jesus* (16mm, color, 10 minutes, produced by CBS)—a film showing Jesus' life in art works; and *Tomorrow's Newspaper* (16mm, b&w, 11 minutes, produced by Zagreb Films)—a film showing distressing aspects of today's society. (**Note:** Show the films with the sound turned off. You may want to start the second film at a point after a scene depicting nudity.) For information on film rentals, see "Movies" in Part Three of this book.

• The musical selection "The Carriage of the Cross" is from the Decca album of Alfred Newman's score for the movie *The Robe*.

• The song "The Sound of Silence" is from Simon and Garfunkel's Columbia album *Greatest Hits*.

• There are many recordings of Ralph Vaughan Williams' "Fantasia on a Theme of Thomas Tallis." Check with a local record store.

This service is adapted from a service on pages 235-236 of *Youth Workers' Handbook*, by Steve Clapp and Jerry O. Cook (C-4 Resources, 1983).

WORSHIP SERVICE NO. 2: "MORNING HAS BROKEN"
(Easter Sunrise Service)

The Prelude: Soft Music by Guitars and/or Other Instruments

The Call to Worship *(responsively)*
Christ is risen!
Christ is risen, indeed!
Let us celebrate the Resurrection as we worship God together!

The Hymn of Praise: "Morning Has Broken"

The Affirmation of Faith *(unison)*
We believe in God, the creator of life and the giver of all good gifts.
We believe in Jesus the Christ, the one who defeated death and arose to new
  life.
We believe in the Holy Spirit, the spirit of truth that lives in us even
  today.
We believe in the church, the caring community that carries on the work
  of Jesus in the world.
We know that God loves us, and we are unafraid.
  We believe in new life—both in this world and in the world to come.
  We face the future without fear,
  Through Jesus Christ, our Lord. Amen.

The Gloria Patri

The Reading from the Old Testament: Isaiah 25:1, 6-9 *(Today's English Version)*

The Offering
  Solo: "Easter Means There's Nothing Left to Fear" (No. 50)

The Doxology

The Prayer of Dedication *(unison)*
O God, we are happy to be here! We celebrate the joy of this Easter season! We praise you for your presence in the mind-boggling events of that first Easter day!

As the sun rises on our celebration of the Resurrection, we pray for the dawning of a new day in our lives. Fill us with faith and give us the gift of new life.

Take our gifts and our lives and use them for your purposes, so that all people may know Jesus as their Lord and experience the joy of Easter. Amen.

The Silent Meditation

The Lord's Prayer *(unison)*

The Hymn of Preparation: "The Lord of the Dance"

The Reading from the New Testament: John 20:11-21 *(Today's English Version)*

The Interpretation of the Word: "The Easter Hope"

The Celebration of the Joy of Easter: Launching of Balloons

The Prayer for New Life *(unison)*
O God, as we launch these balloons, we lift up our hearts and our spirits! We pause and look beyond the distress and the dullness of everyday life. We see the vision of a new day and the wonder of a new way of life.

As Christ arose from the dead, help us to rise above the pain and despair that cloud our horizons. Fill our hearts with the hope and joy of Easter, so that we may find new life in Jesus our Lord. Amen.

The Hymn of Proclamation: "You Can Tell the World"

The Going Forth (*responsively*)
Christ is risen!
Christ is risen, indeed!
You have received the news of the Resurrection. You have celebrated the joy of Easter. You have prayed for new life.
We have heard the good news of God's victory over death. We have a new vision of how good life can be.
Then go forth as new people to live your lives in the joy of the Easter hope!
Amen and Amen!

The Postlude: Loud, Joyful Music by Guitars and/or Other Instruments

* * * * * * * * *

Notes

• **Hymns and Solo.** All of the hymns and the suggested solo may be found in *The Genesis Songbook.*

• **Glori Patri and Doxology.** These selections may be found in *The Genesis Songbook.* The numbers in the service refer to this collection.

• **Balloons.** Helium-filled balloons may be purchased from many party shops. Some welders' supply companies rent helium tanks and sell suitable balloons.

• **Prelude and Postlude.** It is recommended that Easter-related musical selections be used.

• **Interpretation of the Word.** It is recommended that three persons give "mini-sermons" on "The Easter Hope." These talks should focus on the Easter event and signs of hope that speakers see in their own lives and in the world. You may want to include participants' expressions of hope from Worship Service No. 20: "The Hope of the World" in the weekly services section of this book.

WORSHIP SERVICE NO. 3: "FROM GENERATION TO GENERATION"

THE GATHERING

The Prelude

The Sharing: Concerns and Celebrations, Announcements, Opportunities for Service

The Call to Worship *(to be said by the worship leader)*
This is the day that God has made!
It is a time for living and rejoicing!
Let us worship God as we celebrate this day and all the days of our lives.

THE SERVICE OF PRAISE

The Hymn of Praise: "All People That on Earth Do Dwell"

The Affirmation of Faith *(unison)*
We believe in God, the creator of life and the giver of all good gifts.
We believe in Jesus the Christ, the one who defeated death and arose to new
life.
We believe in the Holy Spirit, the spirit of truth that lives in us even
today.
We believe in the church, the caring community that carries on the work
of Jesus in the world.
We know that God loves us, and we are unafraid.
We believe in new life—both in this world and in the world to come.
We face the future without fear,
Through Jesus Christ, our Lord. Amen.

The Gloria Patri

THE SERVICE OF CONFESSION

The Call to Confession *(to be said by the worship leader)*
Let us confess our sins to Almighty God.

The Prayer of Confession *(unison)*
O God, we know that you want us to live in harmony with one another. We know that you call us to a life-style based on loving, caring, accepting, forgiving.

We confess, O God, that we have not always cared for one another as we should. We have shielded ourselves from the needs of others. We have inflicted hurts. We have harbored grudges. We have refused to forgive.

O God, forgive us for our failures, our errors, our sins.

Open our eyes, so that we may see the needs of our neighbors. Open our ears, so that we may hear the pleas for help. Open our hearts, so that we may heal the hurts. Open our lives, so that you may live in us, through Christ our Lord. Amen.

The Words of Hope and Assurance *(to be said by the worship leader)*
1 John 1:5, 7 *(Today's English Version)*

THE SERVICE OF THANKSGIVING

The Reading from the Psalter: Psalms 145:1-7 *(Today's English Version)*

The Call to Thanksgiving *(to be said by the worship leader)*
   Let us worship God with our offerings.

The Offering

The Doxology

The Prayer of Dedication *(unison)*
   O God, we thank you for all of your good gifts. You have blessed us with food and clothing, money and possessions, families and friends, talents and abilities.
   We offer these gifts of money to you as visible signs of our thankfulness. Use these offerings and our lives for your purposes, so that your will may be done both here and throughout the world. Amen.

THE SERVICE OF THE WORD

The Reading from the Old Testament: Jeremiah 1:4-8 *(Today's English Version)*

The Silent Meditation

The Lord's Prayer *(unison)*

The Hymn of Preparation: "Christ, From Whom All Blessings Flow"

The Reading from the New Testament: Matthew 18:1-5 *(Today's English Version)*

The Interpretation of the Word
   1. "What Can Adults Learn From Young Persons?"
   2. "What Can Young Persons Learn From Adults?"
   3. "How Can Adults and Young Persons Work Together as Christians?"

THE SERVICE OF DEDICATION

The Hymn of Dedication: "Blest Be the Tie That Binds"

The Benediction *(to be said by the worship leader)*
   Go forth to live your lives as God directs you! Amen.

The Postlude

* * * * * * * * *

PART THREE: ADDITIONAL RESOURCES

ADDITIONAL HYMNS AND SERVICE MUSIC

This section consists of two parts: (1) a collection of original folk hymns and service music (a term designating standard worship components such as the Gloria Patri, the Doxology, and so forth); and (2) additional ideas on service music.

Come On and Celebrate!

(For Elizabeth Allison Cook)

Piano or Autoharp: Play chords as written.
Guitar: Capo 3rd; play in D.

Words and music by JERRY O. COOK

106

New Circles

(For optional Introduction, see page 2, last line)

Words and music by JERRY O. COOK

(M.M. ♩ = ca. 138)

VERSES GUITAR

1. I'm sur-round-ed by cir-cles— They're ev-'ry-where that I
2. Drops of rain on my win-dow And sport-y wheels on our
3. Now let's sing a-bout cir-cles That aren't so mat-ter of

look: Balls and rings and cir-cly things like rip-ples in a
cars, Drums and plums and round-ed things like shin-y tops on
fact— Si-lent ones that say a lot a-bout how peo-ple

brook. The world's a great big cir-cle, it's just like a fer-ris
jars— The world is full of cir-cles, we see them ev-'ry
act: For love can make a cir-cle and cir-cles are made by

(Optional ending: Repeat last 2 bars of Chorus and fade)

you and me, ___ cir-cles that nev-er end.

Optional Introduction and/or Interlude:
As Introduction: Play twice.
As Interlude: Play once.

New Circles - 2

SING THIS SONG AND CELEBRATE
(For Katharine Sumner Cook)

Words and Music by Jerry O. Cook

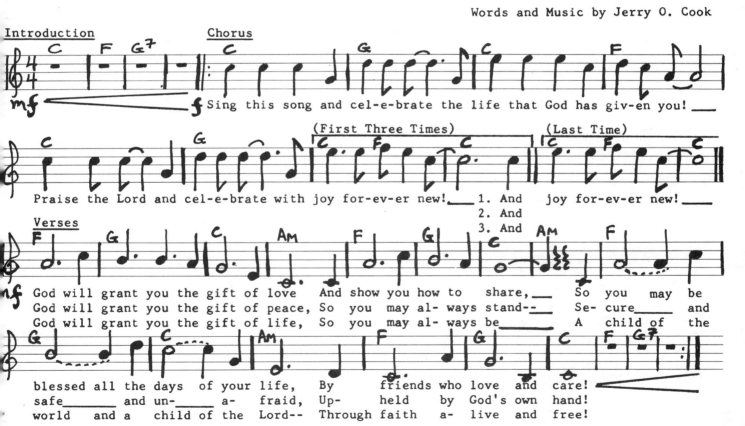

Introduction   **Chorus**

Sing this song and cel-e-brate the life that God has giv-en you! ___

(First Three Times)   (Last Time)

Praise the Lord and cel-e-brate with joy for-ev-er new! ___ 1. And joy for-ev-er new! ___
2. And
3. And

Verses

God will grant you the gift of love And show you how to share, ___ So you may be
God will grant you the gift of peace, So you may al- ways stand-- ___ Se- cure ___ and
God will grant you the gift of life, So you may al- ways be ___ A child of the

blessed all the days of your life, By friends who love and care!
safe ___ and un- ___ a- fraid, Up- held by God's own hand!
world and a child of the Lord-- Through faith a- live and free!

109

SONG FOR A FRIEND

(For Allison)

Words and music by JERRY O. COOK

110

A Song of the Spirit

Words and music by JERRY O. COOK

A Song to Celebrate Myself

Words and Music by JERRY O. COOK

1. I'll sing this song __ to cel-e-brate my-self; __ I'll sing this song with pride; __ What-ev-er I am __ is what God made, __ And I have noth-ing to hide; For __ God made me and God made you, __ And God makes no mis-takes! __ So __ be __ your-self, __ and I'll be me; __ That's all it real-ly takes.

2. I don't have to be __ a plas-tic per-son, All shin-y and all bright. __ I don't have to have __ a pub-lic self; __ The self in-side is all right; So __ I'll af-firm just what I am, And pro-claim my per-son-hood, __ For there's no-one __ else __ in the world like me, __ And what I am __ is good.

3. And if I trav-eled the __ world a-round, And learned ev-'ry-one by name, __ I would-n't __ find __ in th[e] whole wide world __ Two peo-ple just __ the same. But I'd find a great va-ri-e-ty __ Through-out the hu-man race, __ For __ ev-'ry-one's __ spec-ial __ in God's world, __ And ev-'ry-one has a place.

4. So sing this song __ and cel-e-brate your-self; __ Oh, sing this song with pride. __ What-ev-er you are __ is what God made, __ And you have noth-ing to hide; For __ God made me and God made you, __ And God makes no mis-takes! __ So __ be __ your-self, __ and I'll be me; __ That's all it real-ly takes.

(guitar: repeat ad lib and fade)

The Spirit of the Lord

Words and Music by JERRY O. COOK

CHORUS: *with a driving beat (M.M. ♩ = ca. 85-90)*

The Spir - it of the Lord is up - on us, _____ For he has giv - en his com - mand: _____ Take good news to the poor, and set the cap - tives free, And help the op - pressed in the land. _____

VERSES: *lighter, more lyrical*

1. Je - sus stood up in the tem - ple one day And read from the proph - et's word: _____ The Spir - it of the Lord is up - on me to - day And on all who would call me their Lord! _____

2. Je - sus be - friend - ed the need - y and poor. He healed _____ the blind and the lame. _____ But much great - er things than these _____ he said we could do If we'd on - ly be - lieve in his name! _____

3. Our world to - day has its need - y and poor, Its vic - tims of ha - tred and war. _____ Our mis - sion is clear, and our time is to - day; _____ So what are we wait - ing for? _____

113

Tear Down the Walls

Words and music by JERRY O. COOK

114

The Call to Worship

Music by Jerry O. Cook

Moderate tempo

The Lord is in his ho-ly tem-ple, The Lord is in his ho-ly tem-ple; Let all the earth keep si - lence, keep si - lence be-fore ____ him. A - - - men.

The Lord's Prayer

Music by Jerry O. Cook

Slowly

Our Fa - ther, who art in Heav - en; Hal - low - ed be thy name. Thy king-dom come, thy will ____ be done, On earth as it is in heav - en. Give us this day our dai - ly bread, And for-give us our debts, as se for - give our debt - ors, as we for - give our debt - ors, And lead us not in - to temp - ta - tion, but de - liv - er us from e - vil, For

Thine — is the king - dom and the pow - er — and the glo - ry, for - ev - er, for-

ev - er, for - ev - er. A - men. A - - - men.

(**alternate)

-give us our tres - pass - es, as we for - give — those who tres - pass a - gainst us, And

The Gloria Patri

Music by Jerry O. Cook

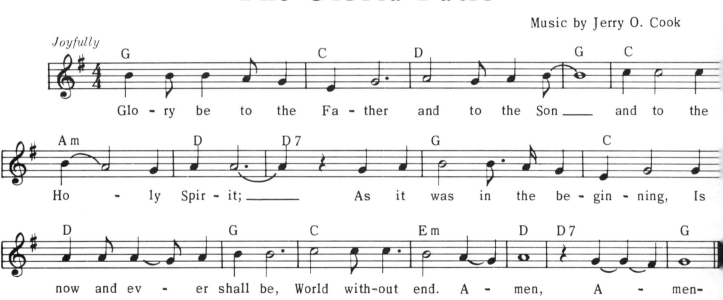

Glo - ry be to the Fa - ther and to the Son — and to the

Ho - ly Spir - it; — As it was in the be - gin - ning, Is

now and ev - er shall be, World with-out end. A - men, A - men-

116

The Apostles' Creed

Music by Jerry O. Cook

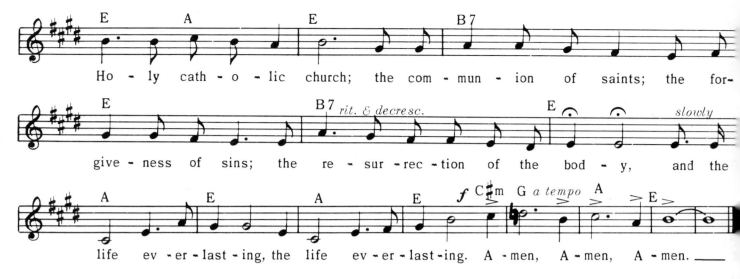

Ho - ly cath - o - lic church; the com - mun - ion of saints; the forgive - ness of sins; the re - sur - rec - tion of the bod - y, and the
life ev - er - last - ing, the life ev - er - last - ing. A - men, A - men, A - men.

The Doxology

Music by Jerry O. Cook

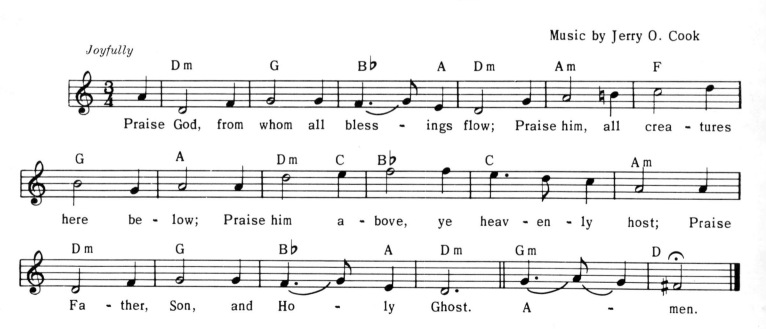

Praise God, from whom all bless - ings flow; Praise him, all crea - tures
here be - low; Praise him a - bove, ye heav - en - ly host; Praise
Fa - ther, Son, and Ho - ly Ghost. A - men.

118

The Preface to the Sanctus
(PART ONE)

Music by Jerry O. Cook

It is ver-y meet, right, ____ and our bound-en du-ty ____
____ That ____ we should at all times and in all pla-ces give ____ thanks un-to Thee, O ____
Lord, Ho - ly Fa - ther, Al - might-y ev - er - last - ing God.

The Preface to the Sanctus
(PART TWO)

Music by Jerry O. Cook

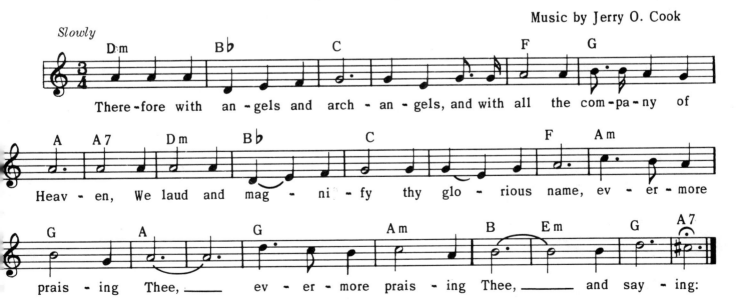

There -fore with an -gels and arch - an - gels, and with all the com-pa-ny of
Heav - en, We laud and mag - ni - fy thy glo - rious name, ev - er - more
prais - ing Thee, ____ ev - er - more prais - ing Thee, ____ and say - ing:

The Sanctus

Lively; Joyfully

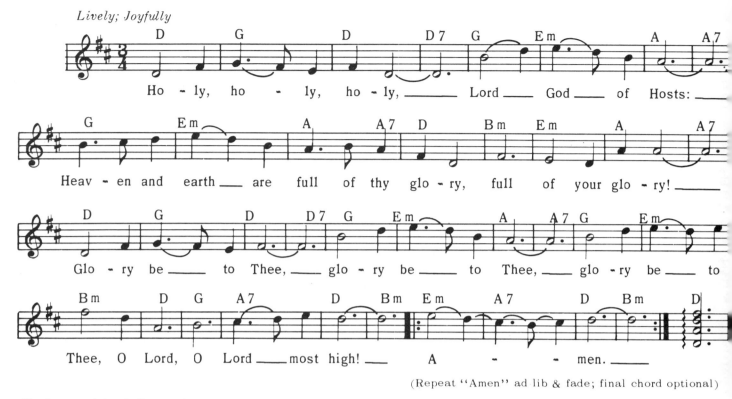

Ho - ly, ho - ly, ho - ly, ____ Lord ____ God ____ of Hosts: ____

Heav - en and earth ____ are full of thy glo - ry, full of your glo - ry! ____

Glo - ry be ____ to Thee, ____ glo - ry be ____ to Thee, ____ glo - ry be ____ to

Thee, O Lord, O Lord ____ most high! ____ A - - men. ____

(Repeat "Amen" ad lib & fade; final chord optional)

The Prayer of Humble Access

Moderately - Gentle Folk tempo

Music by Jerry O. Cook

We do not pre - sume to come to this ____ thy

ta - ble, O mer - ci - ful Lord, Trust - ing in our own right - eous - ness, ____ But

in thy man - i - fold and great mer - cies. We are ____ not worth - y so

much as to gath - er up the crumbs, ____ The crumbs un - der thy ta - ble. the ____

120

crumbs un - der thy ta - ble. But __ Thou art __ the same Lord, the Lord, whose

prop - er - ty __ is al - ways to have mer - cy, is __ al - ways to __ have mer - cy.

Grant us there - fore, gra - cious Lord, __ so to par - take of this sac - ra - ment, of this

sac - ra - ment of thy Son, thy Son, Je - sus Christ, That we __ may walk

in new - ness of life, may __ grow in - to his like - ness, __ (oh, yes) grow in - to his

(At asterisk, begin gradual crescendo & movement toward a driving "rock" feeling in the final bars.)

Music copyrighted © 1973 by Jerry O. Cook

The Agnus Dei

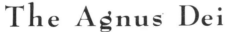

Music by Jerry O. Cook

O Lamb of God, O Lamb __ of God, that

tak - est a - way the sins of the world, Have mer - cy, Have mer - cy up-

on us, O, have mer - cy up - on __ us. O Lamb of God, O Lamb __ of

121

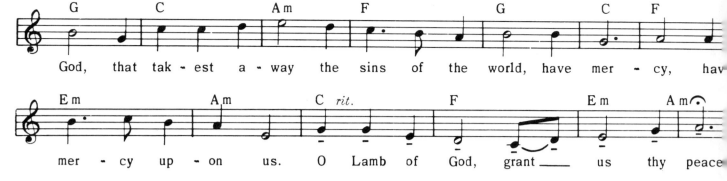

God, that tak-est a-way the sins of the world, have mer-cy, hav[e]

mer-cy up-on us. O Lamb of God, grant ___ us thy peace

Suggestions for Performance:
(1) Solo - bass notes for accmpt.
(2) Choir - chords for accmpt.
(3) All - chords for accmpt.
    Add harmony ad lib on #3

The Words of Administration

Music by Jerry O. Cook

Slowly; Reverently

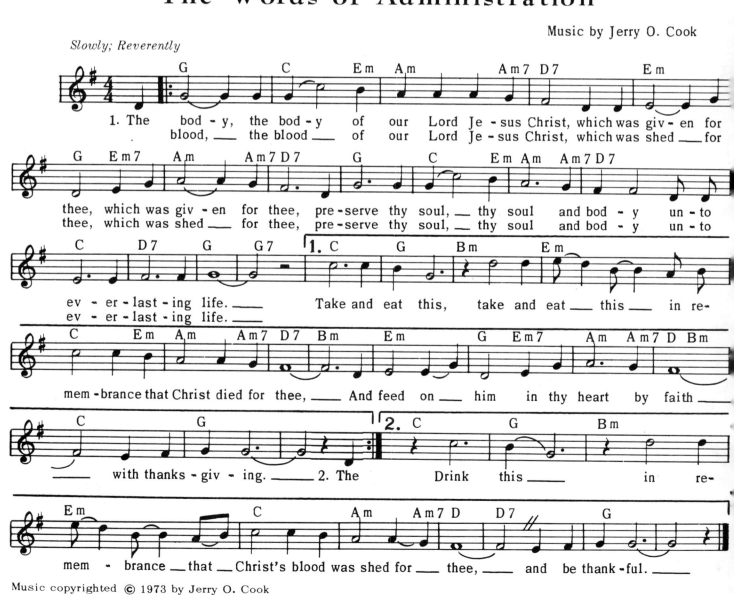

1. The bod-y, the bod-y of our Lord Je-sus Christ, which was giv-en for
   blood, ___ the blood ___ of our Lord Je-sus Christ, which was shed ___ for

thee, which was giv-en for thee, pre-serve thy soul, ___ thy soul and bod-y un-to
thee, which was shed ___ for thee, pre-serve thy soul, ___ thy soul and bod-y un-to

ev-er-last-ing life. ___ Take and eat this, take and eat ___ this ___ in re-
ev-er-last-ing life. ___

mem-brance that Christ died for thee, ___ And feed on ___ him in thy heart by faith ___

___ with thanks-giv-ing. ___ 2. The Drink this ___ in re-

mem-brance ___ that ___ Christ's blood was shed for ___ thee, ___ and be thank-ful. ___

The Benediction

Music by Jerry O. Cook

ADDITIONAL IDEAS ON SERVICE MUSIC

The following list gives some additional ideas on service music that may be used in worship with youth:

Call to Worship
- "With What Will You Come Before the Lord?" by John Ylvisaker *(Songbook for Saints and Sinners,* no. 30).
- "Come Praise, Alleluia," by Gregory Miller *(Songbook for Saints and Sinners,* no. 50).
- "Come, Share the Spirit," by Kent Schneider *(Exodus Songbook,* no. 32).
- "Prepare Ye (TheWay of the Lord)," by Stephen Schwartz. From the musical *Godspell.* Songbook copyrighted © 1971 by Valando Music Inc. & New Cadenza Music Corp. Executive Distributor: Valando Music Inc., 1700 Broadway, New York, NY 10019.

Prayer of Invocation
- "Kum Ba Yah"—an African folk song *(Songbook for Saints and Sinners,* no. 19; *The Genesis Songbook,* no. 46; also found in many camp songbooks).

Doxology
- "Doxology," by Richard Avery and Donald Marsh *(Songbook for Saints and Sinners,* no. 31; *The Genesis Songbook,* no. 55; *Avery and Marsh Songbook,* no. 2).
- "Gentle Doxology," by Richard Avery and Donald Marsh *(Avery and Marsh Songbook,* no. 4).
- "Thanks Be to God," an alternative Doxology by John Ylvisaker *(Songbook for Saints and Sinners,* no. 6). This song may also be sung to the tune of the old song "Windy" by the group The Association.
- *Alternative Ideas for the Doxology: (1) Alternative Words:* Some people prefer to change the words of the Doxology in order to eliminate the masculine references to God. Here is an example:

> *Praise God, from whom all blessings flow;*
> *Praise God, all creatures here below;*
> *Praise God above, ye heavenly host:*
> *Creator, Son and Holy Ghost.*

There have also been some attempts to eliminate the somewhat ambiguous word "Ghost." One such attempt produced this version:

> *Praise God, from whom all blessings flow;*
> *Praise God, all creatures here below;*
> *Praise God above, so all may hear it:*
> *Creator, Son, and Holy Spirit.*

(2) Alternative Tunes: The Doxology is a Common Meter stanza (usually designated by CM); it has a very popular metrical pattern: eight syllables to each line. This same metrical pattern is found in many songs, which means that—with a little creativity—you can sing the Doxology to many alternative tunes. Some examples: "Love Is Blue"; "Jamaica Farewell"; "Hernando's Hideaway."

Gloria Patri
- "Gloria Patri," by Richard Avery and Donald Marsh *(Songbook for Saints and Sinners,* no. 41; *Avery and Marsh Songbook,* no. 3).
- "Gentle Gloria Patri," by Richard Avery and Donald Marsh *(Avery and Marsh Songbook,* no. 5).
- "Gloria Patri," an alternative Gloria Patri by Carlton Young *(The Genesis Songbook,* no. 71. Change "mankind" to "of us."
- *Alternative Words for the Gloria Patri:* Some people prefer to change the words of the Gloria Patri in order to eliminate the masculine references to God. Here is an example:

Glory to the Creator and to the Son and to the Holy Ghost;
As it was in the beginning, is now, and ever shall be,
    world without end. Amen.

There have also been some attempts to eliminate the somewhat ambiguous word "Ghost." This version is an example:

Glory to the Creator and to the Son and to the Holy Spirit;
As it was in the beginning, is now, and ever shall be,
    world without end. Amen.

Call to Prayer
- "It's Me, O Lord," a traditional spiritual (*Songbook for Saints and Sinners*, no. 3; also found in many camp songbooks).

The Lord's Prayer
- "The Lord's Prayer," by Sister Janet Mead (*Exodus Songbook*, no. 46).
- "The Lord's Prayer," by Carlton Young (*The Genesis Songbook*, no. 14).
- "Our Father," an alternative Lord's Prayer with some very interesting words; by Joe Wise (*Pockets*, page 22).

Creed
- "Nicene Creed," by Herbert G. Draesal, Jr. (*Songbook for Saints and Sinners*, no. 38).

Agnus Dei [O Lamb of God]
- "Agnus Dei," by Herbert G. Draesel, Jr. (*The Genesis Songbook*, no. 59).

Benediction
- "Shalom Chaverim [Farewell, Friends]," a traditional Israeli round (*Songbook for Saints and Sinners*, no. 70; *The Genesis Songbook*, no. 68; also found in many camp songbooks).
- "Go and Be Happy," by Richard Avery and Donald Marsh (*The Genesis Songbook*, no. 70).
- "Dona Nobis Pacem [Give Us Peace]," by Ray Repp (*Exodus Songbook*, no. 45).
- "Peace, My Friends," by Ray Repp (*The Genesis Songbook*, no. 74). Change each "all men" to "you all" and "brothers" to "people."
- "You Are the Salt of the Earth," by Richard Avery and Donald Marsh (*Exodus Songbook*, no. 50).
- "Peace," by Gregory Norbet (*Locusts and Wild Honey*, no. 12). Change "all mankind" to "ev'ryone" and "all men" to "people."
- "Friends With You," by Bill Danoff and Taffy Nivert. From the songbook *Aerie: John Denver*. Copyrighted © 1971 by Cherry Lane Music. Sole Selling Agent in the USA: Criterion Music Corp., 17 West 60th St., New York, NY 10023.
- "Forever Young," by Bob Dylan. From the songbook *Joan Baez: From Every Stage*. Copyrighted © 1976 by Almo Publications, 1358 North La Brea, Hollywood, CA 90028.

MOVIES

With the exception of the movie *Portrait of Grandpa Doc* (marked in the listing below with an asterisk), all of the movies recommended in this book may be rented from Ecu-Film and/or Mass Media Ministries. Those available from Ecu-Film are marked *E*; those available from Mass Media Ministries are marked *M*; those available from both Ecu-Film and Mass Media Ministries are marked *EM*.

Addresses for these two suppliers are as follows:

Ecu-Film
810 Twelfth Avenue, South
Nashville, Tennessee 37203
(800-251-4091 *or* 615-242-6277)

Mass Media Ministries
2116 North Charles Street
Baltimore, Maryland 21218
(301-727-3270)

The following is a listing of films recommended in this book:

American Time Capsule (E)
And Then (M)
Angel and Big Joe (EM)
The Antkeeper (M)
Baptism, Sacrament of Belonging (E)
Because They Care (E)
Because This Is Where They Live (E)
Beggar at the Gates (E)
Beginning Now (EM)
Bill Cosby on Prejudice (E)
Bonhoeffer: A Life of Challenge (EM)
The Cave (E)
Celebrate Church Alive (E)
Celebrate Yourself (E)
Christ Is Born (E)
Christmas Bus (E)
Church in the World (E)
A Clown Is Born (EM)
The Coming of the Stranger (EM)
The Dancing Prophet (E)
Diet for a Small Planet (E)
The Eighth Day (M)
Eucharist (Holy Communion) (E)
Everyone, Everywhere (E)
The Face of Jesus (E)
Feelings (EM)
A Friendly Game (EM)
From Whom All Blessings Flow (E)
A Fuzzy Tale (EM)
The Gift (E)

The Hat (EM)
How Good Life Can Be (E)
How's Your New Friend? (E)
Hunger (E)
Leisure (E)
Let the Rain Settle It (E)
Light Shines in the Darkness (E)
The Longest Stride (M)
Luke Was There (EM)
The Mark of the Clown (EM)
Miscommunications (M)
Nail (E)
Oh Happy Day (EM)
One Who Was There (EM)
The Parable (EM)
Peege (E)
Portrait of Grandpa Doc*
Search, Christian Encounter (E)
The Shopping Bag Lady (EM)
The String (M)
That's Life (M)
Theirs Is the Kingdom (E)
Though I Walk Through the Valley (EM)
Time Structure (EM)
Tomorrow's Newspaper (M)
Transactions (EM)
The Way Home (E)
The Word Is Celebration, Part I (E)
The World of Jesus Christ (M)

*The film *Portrait of Grandpa Doc* may be ordered from the producer: Pyramid Film Producers, P.O. Box 1048, Santa Monica, California 90406.

Film Catalogs

There are many excellent suppliers of films for religious groups. Order catalogues from the following:

Association Films, Association Instructional Materials, 866 Third Avenue, New York, New York 10022.

The Eccentric Circle Cinema Workshop, P.O. Box 1481, Evanston, Illinois 60204.

Ecu-Film, 810 Twelfth Avenue, South, Nashville, Tennessee 37203.

Insight Films, Paulist Productions, P.O. Box 1057, Pacific Palisades, California 90272.

Learning Corporation of America, 711 Fifth Avenue, New York, New York 10022.

Mass Media Ministries, 2116 North Charles Street, Baltimore, Maryland 21218.

Pyramid Film Producers, Box 1048, Santa Monica, California 90406.

TeleKETICS (St. Francis Productions), 1229 South Santee Street, Los Angeles, California 90015.

There are many sources for secular motion pictures. Check in your geographical area and with your local library for several suggestions and compare prices. Many church groups have had good luck with **Swank Motion Pictures,** 6767 Forest Lawn Drive, Hollywood, California 90068.

A SELECTIVE LISTING OF ADDITIONAL WORSHIP RESOURCES

The annotated listing in this section is designed to give guidance in the selection of additional worship resources. Although the list is by no means exhaustive, it does include some of the better worship resources produced in the past few years. Current information on new resources may be found in the *C-4 Ministry Update* or in catalogues, brochures, and so forth, from companies and organizations listed in our "Addresses" section.

Many of these resources may be found in Christian bookstores and supply houses. For Catholic resources, check with a Catholic bookstore in your area. Some resources are available from sources listed in the "Addresses" section. In the case of resources that may be out-of-print, you may be able to borrow copies from your pastor, your Christian education director, your church library, an area denominational resource center, or a local library.

The categories in this listing are as follows: *(1) Songbooks; (2) Worship, Drama, and Clown Ministry; (3) Media; (4) General Resources; and (5) Addresses.*

SONGBOOKS

Abba, Father, by the Reverend Carey Landry (North American Liturgy Resources, 1977).
A superb collection of thirteen songs by a very talented Catholic priest. A recording is available separately from the same publisher.

The Avery and Marsh Songbook, by Richard K. Avery and Donald S. Marsh (Proclamation Productions, 1973).
An excellent collection of original folk hymns. Geared to the church year. Available in a large piano-accompaniment edition and in a small edition with words, melodies, and guitar chord markings.

Close Your Eyes. . . . I Got a Surprise, by Joe Wise (North American Liturgy Resources, 1974).
This exellent collection of some of Joe Wise's songs is designed to be a children's resource. Of the ten songs in this book, however, four may also be used effectively with youth and adults. The four "intergenerational" songs are: "Yes to You, My Lord"; "I Believe in You"; "For Tommy: Thanks for the Chance"; and "Fill It With Sunshine." A recording featuring the composer and a children's chorus is available separately from the publisher.

The Exodus Songbook, edited by Carlton R. Young (Agápe, 1975).
An excellent collection of music for use in innovative worship. Contains modern folk hymns and many pop songs. Available in a large piano-accompaniment edition and in a small edition with words, melodies, and guitar chord markings.

The Genesis Songbook, edited by Carlton R. Young (Agápe, 1973).
An excellent collection of modern folk hymns and some pop songs that can be used in innovative worship. Available in a large piano-accompaniment edition and in a small edition with words, melodies, and guitar chord markings.

Gold, Incense and Myrrh, by Sister Miriam Therese Winter and the Medical Mission Sisters (Vanguard Music, 1971-72).
A collection of twleve contemporary Christmas carols. Some are suitable for congregational singing; others are good solo selections.

Joy Is Like the Rain, by Sister Miriam Therese Winter and the Medical Mission Sisters (Vanguard Music, 1965-66)
A collection of eight very tuneful folk hymns. A recording is available separately on Avant Garde Records.

Listen, by Gregory Norbet and the Monks of Weston Priory (Weston Priory Productions, 1973).
A collection of singable folk hymns for various seasons of the church year.

Locusts and Wild Honey, by Gregory Norbet and the Monks of Weston Priory (Weston Priory Productions, 1971).
More delightful folk hymns from Weston's monks.

A New Commandment, by Joe Wise (Graded Press, 1973).
This songbook comes packaged with a recording in a kit originally designed for use with older elementary children. Almost all of the twelve selections can also be used with youth and adults, however. Order from Cokesbury at one of the addresses given in our "Addresses" section.

Pockets, by Joe Wise (Fontaine House; Pastoral Arts Associates of North America, 1978).
This songbook consists of eight songs for children. For youth workers, it is worth the price just to get Wise's "Our Father," an alternative version of the Lord's Prayer with very interesting words. A recording is available separately from Pastoral Arts Associates of North America.

Songbook for Saints and Sinners, edited by Carlton R. Young (Agápe, 1971).
One of the best standard collections of modern folk hymns and other contemporary music for use in innovative worship. Available in a large piano-accompaniment edition and in a small edition with words, melodies, and guitar chord markings.

Wherever You Go, by Gregory Norbet and the Monks of the Weston Priory (Weston Priory Productions, 1972).
More of those inspiring songs by the Weston monks.

WORSHIP, DRAMA, AND CLOWN MINISTRY

The Banner Book, by Betty Wolfe (Morehouse-Barlow, 1975). 96 pages.
A very good book that gives detailed instructions for banner-making.

Children, Celebrate! Resources for Youth Liturgy, by Sister Maria Rabalais, C.S.J., and Howard Hall (Paulist Press, 1974). 137 pages.
A Catholic resource that is quite usable by Protestants. Contains general guidelines on innovative worship, much modern liturgical material, and some very good appendices (Scripture listings and bibliographies). Designed for use with children and youth, but the youth sections are clearly designated as such.

The Complete Floyd Shaffer Clown Ministry Workshop Kit, by Floyd Shaffer. Produced by Dennis C. Benson.
An excellent resource for persons who want to get into this innovative form of ministry. Six cassettes and a manual. Order from Dennis Benson at address given in our listing of addresses.

Create and Celebrate! by Jay C. Rochelle (Fortress Press, 1971). 124 pages.
A very good book to use in creating worship experiences with youth. Contains chapters on innovative worship, much modern liturgical material, and an excellent ten-page bibliography.

Making Tracks, by Dennis C. Benson (Abingdon Press, 1979). 126 pages.
A superb collection of devotional writings that may be used in individual devotionals or in youth worship services. Order from Dennis Benson at address given in our listing of addresses.

Praise the Lord! by James E. Haas (Morehouse-Barlow, 1974). 32 pages.
A good little book on innovative worship with youth. Contains ideas for eleven services. In some cases, musical ideas should be up-dated.

20 Ways to Use Drama in Teaching the Bible, by Judy Gattis Smith (Griggs Educational Service). 80 pages.
An excellent resource that contains much useful information on how to use drama in Bible study—and in other situations in church-related settings.

Ventures in Worship, edited by David James Randolph (Abingdon Press, 1969, 1970, 1973). 3 volumes. 353 pages (total).

An excellent resource for innovative worship. Contains many contemporary prayers, litanies, orders of worship, and so forth—along with many helpful articles on contemporary worship.

The Workbook of Living Prayer, by Maxie Dunnam (Discipleship Resources—Board of Discipleship of The United Methodist Church, 1974). 138 pages.

An excellent resource for youth (and others!) who want to deepen their prayer life. Provides guidelines and information for a six- to ten-week seminar. Order from Discipleship Resources at address given in our listing of addresses.

MEDIA

Better Media for Less Money! by Donn P. McGuirk (National Teacher Education Project, 1972). 56 pages.

An excellent resource to help you utilize media without going broke! Order from: NTEP at address given in our listing of addresses.

Better Media: Volume II, by Donn P. McGuirk (National Teacher Education Project, 1978). 80 pages.

More of the same! Excellent! Order from: NTEP at address given in our listing of addresses.

Cultural Information Service, P.O. Box 92, New York, New York 10016.

An excellent periodical containing in-depth reviews of books, commercial films, TV programs, pop music recordings, and so forth—with emphasis on the Christian perspective on these media.

Festival, by Lyman Coleman and Ken Curtis (Serendipity House, 1973). 96 pages.

An excellent resource for a church-related group that wants to combine faith exploration with film-making. Divided into three parts: team-building labs; biblical research; and film-making steps.

Gadgets, Gimmicks and Grace: A Handbook on Multimedia in Church and School, by Edward N. McNulty (Abbey Press, 1976). 130 pages.

A very good introduction to the use of media in church-related settings. Has an excellent bibliography.

Getting Started in Film-making, by Lillian Schiff (Sterling Publishing Company, 1978). 96 pages.

A very good primer for persons who are making their first film.

Music and the Young, C-4 Resources, P.O. Box 1408, Champaign, Illinois 61820.

A monthly resource that provides information on relating Christianity to rock music and other aspects of youth culture. Includes ideas on using current pop music in worship with youth.

Slide and Film Making Manual, by Donald Griggs (Griggs Educational Service). 53 pages.

An excellent resource giving detailed information on how to make your own slides and films without a camera.

GENERAL RESOURCES

Alternative Celebrations Catalogue (Alternatives, various dates and editions).

A superb resource for persons who want to be more responsible in the ways that they celebrate holidays, birthdays, and so forth. Includes many ideas that are suitable for use in youth worship services. Order from Alternatives at the address given in our "Addresses" section.

The Basic Encyclopedia for Youth Ministry, by Dennis C. Benson and William E. Wolfe (Group Magazine, 1981).

An excellent resource that covers youth ministry from A to Z (from **aaugh!** to **zits**). Information on sexuality, food for youth groups, retreats, pop music, worship, and much more. Order from Group Magazine at address given in our listing of addresses.

Building an Effective Youth Ministry, by Glenn E. Ludwig (Abingdon, 1979). 125 pages.

An excellent little book that provides a comprehensive view of youth ministry and many helpful specific suggestions. Topics dealt with include: avoiding the wrong questions about youth ministry; a theological framework for youth ministry; myths about youth; the structural issue; programming; youth advisors; administrative ideas; retreats; and additional resources.

Catch the Rainbow, edited by Dave Stone (Abingdon Press).

This is the second volume by Dave Stone and many other youth workers. It contains more creative ideas like those found in *The Complete Youth Ministries Handbook.*

The Complete Youth Ministries Handbook, edited by Dave Stone (Abingdon, 1980).

This is actually Volume I of a two-volume set. Dave and a creative group of people got together to write a complete handbook, and then discovered that one was not enough to do the job. Contains a number of suggestions. This book will probably be of most help to persons working in fairly large churches. You can buy the book itself, or you can order it with two cassette tapes on which Jim Moore conducts an interview with Dave Stone.

Creative Youth Leadership, by Jan Corbett (Judson Press, 1977). 128 pages.

An excellent resource that provides a very good overall view of youth ministry. Divided into four sections: the basics of youth leadership; understanding youth; skills for the experienced youth leader; and problem clinic.

The Exuberant Years: A Guide for Jr. High Leaders, by Ginny Ward Holderness (John Knox Press, 1976). 215 pages.

Absolutely one of the best books on working with junior high youth in the church. Included in this book are sections on: preparing for the encounter; developing a useful structure; planning special events; methods that work; mini-courses; creating your own programs; and much more.

Gaming: The Fine Art of Creating Simulation/Learning Games for Religious Education, by Dennis C. Benson (Abingdon Press, 1971). 64 pages.

An excellent book. Contains detailed instructions for eight superb simulation games and two sound-sheets. Order from Dennis Benson at address given in our listing of addresses.

GROUP Magazine, from Thom Schultz Publications.

This magazine and the special edition for leaders are excellent resources for youth workers in any denomination. The materials are attractive, well prepared, and genuinely ecumenical. You can get a discount if you order subscriptions in bulk. Order from the address in our address listing.

The Group Retreat Book, by Arlo Reichter and others (Group Books, 1983).

A superb book that includes nineteen chapters on retreat planning and thirty-four designs for retreats. Includes some ideas for worship and an excellent listing of various kinds of youth resources.

Hard Times Catalog for Youth Ministry, by Marilyn and Dennis Benson (Group Books, 1982).

An excellent resource containing hundreds of low-cost and no-cost ideas for youth ministry. Includes 75 pages on worship celebrations.

Ideas, edited by Wayne Rice and Mike Yaconelli (Youth Specialties, various copyright dates). More than twenty-five volumes, with additional volumes published each year.

One of the best resources published by the superb Youth Specialties organization. Especially good for recreation and communications ideas. Consists of ideas sent in from youth workers throughout the country. Main divisions of volumes include: crowd breakers; games; special events; creative communication; dramatics; case studies. Order from Youth Specialties at address given in our listing of addresses.

Recycle Catalogue, by Dennis C. Benson (Abingdon Press, 1975). 207 pages.

More than six-hundred creative teaching/learning ideas from Christian educators throughout the country. An excellent resource—with **ten** indexes to help you locate ideas. Order from Dennis Benson at address given in our listing of addresses.

Recycle Catalogue II, by Dennis C. Benson (Abingdon Press, 1977). 158 pages.

More of the same! Excellent! Order from Dennis Benson at address given in our listing of addresses.

Recycle newsletter, c/o Dennis C. Benson, P.O. Box 12811, Pittsburgh, Pennsylvania 15241.

Each issue of this excellent publication contains ideas on Christian education from twenty-five to thirty persons from throughout the country. Published nine times a year.

Retreat Handbook, by Virgil and Lynn Nelson (Judson Press, 1976). 127 pages.

A comprehensive handbook for planning retreats. Many program ideas and activities included.

Serendipity Books, by Lyman Coleman (Word Books, various dates).

These are outstanding resources for group building and relational Bible study. The multiple-choice strategies can grow old with some youth groups, but few resources have proven as stimulating as those by Coleman. Write to WORD for a complete listing of these excellent materials. See the address in our address listing.

Youth Workers' Handbook, by Steve Clapp and Jerry O. Cook (C-4, 1983).

This is the book that Lyle Schaller calls "the best youth worker's book" on the market! It's packed with creative ideas, and we've just revised it again!

ADDRESSES

Abbey Press, St. Meinrad, Indiana 47577
Posters; books; religious jewelry and plaques; and so forth.

Agape, Main Place, Carol Stream, Illinois 60187.
Many collections of modern folk hymns.

Alternatives, 1124 Main St., P.O. Box 1707, Forest Park, Georgia 30051.
Resources on more responsible life-styles.

Argus Communications, Dept. 50, 7440 Natchez Avenue, Niles, Illinois 60648.
Posters; books; audio-visual materials; study courses on the Bible, human relationships, world religions, and so forth.

Dennis C. Benson, P.O. Box 12811, Pittsburgh, Pennsylvania 15241.
Newsletters, cassettes, books, and other resources for Christian education.

C-4 RESOURCES, P.O. Box 1408, Champaign, Illinois 61820.
That's us!!!!! You can get lots of books on youth ministry and a subscription to *Music and the Young.* Also get on the mailing list for our free **C-4 UPDATE.**

Cast-Off Productions, P.O. Box 10, Nashville, Tennessee 37221.
Resources for local church communicators; resources for clown, mime, puppet, and story-telling ministries.

Center for Contemporary Celebration, 119 North 6th Street, Lafayette, Indiana 47901.
Resources for worship and education about worship. Ideas on: music; dance; banners; multi-media; liturgy; and so forth.

Clown Ministry Cooperative, P.O. Box 24023, Nashville, Tennessee 37202.
Clown ministry books, pamphlets, and supplies; and information on workshops.

Cokesbury. Any of the following addresses: (1) 1661 North Northwest Highway, Park Ridge, Illinois 60069 (312-299-4411); (2) 1635 Adrian Road, Burlingame, California 94010 (415-692-3562); (3) 201 Eighth Avenue, South, P.O. Box 801, Nashville, Tennessee 37202 (615-749-6113).

The retail division of The United Methodist Publishing House. Supplier of denominational materials for The United Methodist Church, The Presbyterian Church, and The United Church of Christ. Produces several catalogues including books, records, church and church school supplies and equipment, and other materials. Also operates Cokesbury stores throughout the country.

Contemporary Drama Service, P.O. Box 457-GS, Downers Grove, Illinois 60515.
Resources for drama, musicals, choral readings, readers theater, and so forth.

Discipleship Resources, P.O. Box 840, Nashville, Tennessee 37202. (615-327-2700)
Resources and materials for youth ministry and ministry in general. Though produced by The United Methodist Church, many of these resources and materials are usable by other denominations.

Griggs Educational Service, P.O. Box 363, Livermore, California 94550.
Resources and materials for Christian education. Emphasis on teaching methods and usage of media.

GROUP Magazine, Thom Schultz Publications, Box 481, Loveland, Colorado 80537.
Schultz publishes the excellent **GROUP Magazine** and several other materials for youth ministry.

National Teacher Education Project, 6947 East MacDonald Drive, Scottsdale, Arizona 85253. (602-948-7536)
Resources for church school teachers: books; films; filmstrips; cassettes; and so forth. **Church Teacher** magazine.

North American Liturgy Resources, 2110 West Peoria Avenue, Phoenix, Arizona 85029 (800-528-6043)
Recordings and songbooks (folk hymns). Catholic material, but much of it usable by Protestants.

Office of Communications Education, United Methodist Communications, 810 12th Avenue, South, Nashville, Tennessee 37203.
Brochures and other materials relating to communications in church settings.

Nido R. Qubein and Associates, P.O. Box 5367, High Point, North Carolina 27262.
Newsletter, books, tapes, and other resources for your work with young people.

Pastoral Arts Associates of North America, 4744 West Country Gables Drive, Glendale, Arizona 85306.
Songs by Joe Wise. Excellent musical material for use by children, youth, and adults.

Proclamation Productions, Orange Square, Port Jervis, New York 12771. (914-856-6686)
Folk hymns by Avery and Marsh; and resources for innovative worship.

The United Methodist Publishing House, 201 Eighth Avenue, South, Nashville, Tennessee 37202.
This is the largest religious publishing house in the world and produces many youth ministry resources which can be used across denominational lines. Write for copies of **Youth Planbook, Arena,** and **Youth Leader**.

Weston Priory Productions, Weston, Vermont 05161.
Many songbooks containing modern folk hymns. Excellent materials for use by any denomination.

WORD, Inc., Educational Products Division, 4800 Waco Drive, Waco, Texas 76710.
Serendipity books and many other excellent resources.

Youth Specialties, 1224 Greenfield Drive, El Cajon, California 92021.
Many resources for youth ministry, including: the *Ideas* series; cassettes; **Wittenburg Door** magazine. Sponsors of the annual International Youth Workers' Conventions and seminars throughout the country.